Birds

IN YOUR BACK YARD

Birds

IN YOUR BACK YARD

BY TED S. PETTIT

BIRD DRAWINGS BY *George Greller*
LINE DRAWINGS BY *Donald Ross*

AVENEL BOOKS · NEW YORK

To
Mary, Beth and Ann

Contents

Illustrations

Birds

IN YOUR BACK YARD

CHAPTER 1

BACK YARD BIRDING

Someday soon you can expect to hear of a new bird club—"Bird Watchers Anonymous"—patterned after the older organization with a slightly similar name. Although it is doubtful that overindulgence in bird watching would have the same effect as too much alcohol, you would have a hard time convincing any family which spends the better part of its life waiting for a wandering father to find his way home from his favorite bar—sand bar that is—or swamp.

We cannot speak with too much authority on meanderings from other causes, but we do know that a serious interest in birds causes one to wander considerably, for long periods of time in rather unusual places. During one period in our growth as a birder, we spent every week end on one or more of New York's better land fills (garbage dumps in popular terms). At other times we have waded through the muddiest of mud flats for days on end, or spent our days jumping jetties along Long Island's lengthy shore line—pastimes hardly conducive to regular home habits.

Thus to avoid being enrolled forcibly as a charter member of this new bird club, we have confined our efforts, of recent years, to bird watching in our own yard, and in those of our immediate neighbors. Of course, we slip occasionally, and go off on a round of salt marsh, beach and woodland binges. But by and large, we are satisfied that we have a worthwhile hobby right in our own yard—and one of interest to the rest of the family. In fact, we heartily recommend it to any one else, not too set in his ways or too devoted to peaceful and regular habits. For even birds in your back yard (or the city park or along a golf course) can give rise to many interesting situations.

What Is It Daddy?

Probably the most frequent incident to interrupt the peaceful home atmosphere comes after you have settled down to read the Sunday paper—or to take a short nap after weeding the petunias or hoeing the corn. You have already filled the bird feeders around the yard, and have put fresh water in the bird baths. You have scanned the tree tops, shrubs and ground, and the only birds around are the ever-present English sparrows, starlings or blue jays. You have settled down in peace— the children are playing in the yard—were playing in the yard, because the door slams and in they tiptoe and whisper furtively:

"Daddy, there is a new bird in the feeder. What is it, Daddy?"

At that point you do not care what it is, but you started the whole thing, and that psychologist the other night said you cannot frustrate your children. They will grow up to have unbalanced egos, or something. So you grab your binoculars or field glasses and sneak out to see this new bird. (You have already taught the youngsters all the common birds, so perhaps this may be something unusual.) As you quietly and slowly move down the back steps, the door slams behind you, and four little feet patter down the steps like•little horses on a wooden bridge. But the bird is still there. You focus the glasses and take a look—yes, there *is* a new bird in your yard for that time of year. It is a chipping sparrow.

"Pretty smart kids, you've got there," you think. "Can't fool them. They know the difference . . ."

So you whisper, "It's a chipping sparrow. See it eating the cracked corn."

"Gi'me the glasses," they scream and almost decapitate you as they grab the binoculars that are hanging around your neck.

After each has had a turn, and the glasses are so completely out of focus that you know they cannot even see the house next door, you are ready to go back to the paper. Then comes the climax:

"How do you know it's a chipping sparrow?"

"See the reddish spot on the head? That is the quickest way to tell," you answer patiently.

"I don't see any red spot. Gi'me the glasses again. Show me a picture of it . . ."

And for the next half an hour you try to convince your skeptical little offspring that you know a chipping sparrow when you see one.

Are Those Birds Fighting, Daddy?

But that is nothing to the questions that accompany the coming of spring as surely as the robins.

Of course, the problem is largely one of your own personal conscience. You have an easy way out—but will you take it? We cannot. We must, for some reason, face the truth—even if it means a rather early and frequently repeated lesson in sex education.

For birds are no respecters of time or place, despite the theories of a lady we heard of recently from our County Agent. The good lady had recently moved to the country and immediately set out to raise chickens for eggs. The County Agent noticed that her flock included two roosters. He told her that if all she wanted was eggs—and if she wanted to sell the eggs—it would be better to eat the roosters. Some people are particular about those little red spots in the yolks. But the farmerette had her answer ready. It was perfectly all right, she said. She took the roosters out of the coop every night.

Just as surely as the robins return in the spring, that question will arise: "Are those birds fighting, Daddy?" What will you do? Get your answer ready early, and make it good. And get set for the aftereffects too. You can't tell when they will pop up.

Our daughter was barely in kindergarten when she started asking questions. It started with birds. What is a male? What is a female? Am I a female? Is a bird an animal? What else are animals? Am I an animal? Oh, I am a female mammal—and then to school and the age-old question by a well-meaning

teacher: "What are you going to be when you grow up?"
Answer: "A big female mammal." End of questions, as teacher
exits blushing.

What Do I Do Now?

Of course, bird watching has its less complicated side too.
You may go along for weeks or even months with scarcely a
thing to mar the peace and solitude of your hobby. But neighbors are bound to ask what you are looking at in the top of
that tree, or out in the field, and you have to tell them. Pretty
soon word gets around that you are an expert ornithologist,
and can answer any and all questions about birds.

In the beginning you will only get telephone calls from
people you never heard of, but who know you by reputation:

"I have a bird in my back yard. Can you tell me what it
is? It is all brown."

"How big is it?"

"Oh, like a sparrow, or maybe a crow. It is all brown
streaks down the front. There are five or six of them on the
grass."

"Are they starlings?"

"No. I know starlings. They're black."

"Yes, but maybe they're young starlings. Young starlings
are brown, and streaked on the breast."

"Yes. They look like starlings. But I didn't know that
young starlings are differently colored. That is what they
are—there are a couple of old ones with them."

Then your reputation is made. So get ready for the next
series of calls—either by telephone or in person.

"I have a baby bird that fell out of the nest. You know all

about birds. We thought you'd like to have it. We'll watch you take care of it."

If you are smart, you will suddenly remember a previous engagement over in the next county and rush off with profuse apologies.

For one bird leads to another, and injured birds follow young birds—and a back yard, garage or cellar aviary takes a lot of time and trouble. One bird hobbyist we have met got to the stage where she had to hire neighborhood boys to collect insects, dig worms, and collect wild fruits to feed the dozen or so birds that accumulated in her house. Vacations, week-end trips—even a shopping day in the city were out of the question. Birds must eat, and are more demanding than your own infant with its five or six feedings a day. Some birds have to be fed, just like a baby—but there is one consolation: they do not have to be burped, or changed. Those functions they take care of themselves—always when it is least convenient and in the least appropriate place. Did you ever try housebreaking a bird?

Another friend of ours unwittingly found himself playing host to about a thousand ducks a day for some two or three months a year. It sounds nice, doesn't it? A thousand ducks out in your back yard? Mallards, blacks, baldpates, shovellers, pintails, teal and woodducks are certainly beautiful to watch as they swim around, or drop in on set wings so close you can watch the twisting of their wings as they control their flight. But did you ever try to feed a thousand ducks? It takes hundreds of pounds of corn a month, and that much corn can be expensive. And it all started so innocently.

It all began with a half-dozen mallards purchased from a

game farm to add beauty to a small natural pond. These ducks were fed daily from spring until fall. Then the duck migration started. These tame birds decoyed a few wild birds which, undisturbed, fed with the tame birds. As cold weather set in, and more ducks moved south, more and more stopped in at the pond—some for a day or two, some for the balance of the winter. Soon the ducks numbered a thousand or more and all were hungry. Of course, they would have moved on if food had not been provided. But it seemed a shame to drive away that many birds when they could be made to stay.

Even such a harmless hobby as feeding birds can lead to many complications—but not many people have opportunities to get so involved. Most of us settle for juncos, sparrows, jays, nuthatches, or grosbeaks—which do not eat as much as ducks, fortunately.

To be sure, a bird watching hobby is not all that way. Thousands of bird hobbyists just go through life enjoying their little feathered friends, with not a care in the world. But when we ride a hobby, we really ride it—which probably accounts for the experiences we have had.

Frankly, we turn a little green at the reaction of some of our bird watching friends. Anthropomorphizing, the dictionary calls it. Our terms are less scientific but much more expressive. But why some people describe the behavior of the birds they see in a goose pimple-raising baby talk, with constant references to mamma bird and poppa bird, and itty, bitty baby, is beyond us. Those people take keen delight in attributing human qualities to birds. And we feel like carrying out a process used by some birds in feeding their young —or as a defense mechanism—regurgitating. Not nice perhaps, but when we see some of the work done by serious amateur bird watchers, we lose a lot of respect for those people who spend their time interpretating birds' actions in the light of what they think birds think.

Far be it from us to suggest that everyone should be a scientist. There are many good reasons for watching birds— not the least of which is for the pure personal enjoyment of nature at its best, in color and song. Everyone has his own reason, and knows the degree to which he wants to follow any particular hobby. But may the Lord deliver us from the "dickey-birder" who starts out the story:

"I saw the cutest thing. The mamma robin went chirp, chirp (accompanied by arm flapping, and a loud and poor imitation of a robin's alarm note) and away flew the itty babies. And then the big bad cat came around the rose bush . . ." That is when we remember an urgent engagement.

Other Side of The Story

But there is another side to bird watching that makes it such a fascinating hobby. First of all it is a year 'round hobby, with just as much fun in winter as in summer—in spring as in fall—especially if you concentrate in your own yard. It has the same thrill that comes to the collector as he finds a rare specimen to add to his collection—the same thrill that comes to fishermen when the big one does not get away—the same thrill that comes to the flower grower who succeeds in growing something new. And depending upon the extent to which you ride the hobby, it can have the same thrill of accomplishment that comes to a scientist who completes a lengthy project. For whether you watch birds for the aesthetic enjoyment you get; whether you compete with neighbors or friends to see which yard attracts the most birds for a year; whether you keep records of the birds you see for several years to collect migration, breeding and other data; or whether you combine photography with an interest in birds—you have a hobby for all the family, for every month of the year.

Bird Watching Equipment

Like most hobbies, bird watching requires equipment, and like some hobbies, this equipment may be as expensive or inexpensive as you want to make it.

Most important, especially if you are a beginner, is a good field guide to the birds of your area. For anyone living east of the Rocky Mountains, there are two good books that are recommended. First is Roger Tory Peterson's *Field Guide to the Birds*. This guide, with both black and white and colored illustrations, contains illustrations of all birds—songbirds, hawks, owls, shorebirds, gulls, terns and waterfowl. Second is Richard H. Pough's *Audubon Bird Guide*. The advantage of this book is that all illustrations are in color and appear in one section of the book, with cross-references to verbal descriptions.

For those living in the Southwestern or Western part of the United States, Mr. Peterson's *Field Guide to Western Birds* is recommended. Like its eastern counterpart, this pocket guide contains black and white and colored illustrations and describes all groups of birds.

In addition, many states publish books or pamphlets on the birds of that state. The best plan is to write to the State Conservation Commission, State Museum, State Commerce Department, in the state capitol, and ask if such books are published for your state (or neighboring states). Other books are listed in the bibliography.

Also important for successful bird watching is a pair of field glasses or binoculars. It is difficult to recommend any particular glass—because of the many kinds available, and because of the cost range. Perhaps it is better to consider the desirable features of the ideal bird glass and then to select the one that has the most number of these features.

How To Select Binoculars

Probably the most desirable feature of binoculars for birds is the light-gathering ability. Enough time is spent watching birds in early morning, on dark days, in deep woods and at other times and places when light is not of the best, to make light-gathering ability important. This light-gathering ability of the glass is the factor that enables you to see color in birds —and that is one good reason that many people enjoy watching birds.

To determine the relative light-gathering ability of binoculars divide the diameter of the objective lens by the power and "square" the number you get. In other words, the light-gathering power of a 6x30 glass is 25. ($30 \div 6 = 5$. $5 \times 5 = 25$.) The 6 represents the power of the glass—meaning that a robin seen through a six power glass seems six times closer than it is. The 30 represents the diameter in millimeters of the objective lens or the lens away from the eye.

The most common formulas for binoculars are: 6x24; 6x30; 7x35; 8x24; 8x30; 7x50; 9x35; 8x40; 10x35; 10x40; 10x50. As far as power and light-gathering ability are concerned probably the best combination for bird binoculars are 7x35; 7x50; 8x40; 10x50. Other sizes are perfectly satisfactory, depending upon individual choice and preference.

Another important factor in a bird glass is the "field"— that is the width covered by the glasses at a given distance, usually one thousand yards. Only manufacturers can give you that information. Usually, the higher the power, the less is the field. But even low power glasses sometimes have narrow fields; and some higher power glasses have wider fields.

Most manufacturers represent the width in terms of yards at one thousand yards. But some represent the width in feet covered at one thousand yards. Watch for this measurement when comparing glasses.

Other factors depending upon individual makes that are important are rugged construction, and resistance to moisture and dust. About the best check on these factors is the reputation of the manufacturer. In this regard, it is suggested that the prospective purchaser beware of so-called war binoculars. Some glasses brought home from Japan and Germany were very inferior to American-made glasses—and purchasing them would be false economy. It has been said by reputable dealers that even the German glasses made today in Germany are far inferior to glasses manufactured before the war, despite the old and very fine reputation of the manufacturers.

Size and weight are also important considerations. If most observing is to be done in the yard, or where considerable walking is not necessary, size and weight does not make too much difference. You can usually find a place to rest your elbows to steady a heavy glass. But if you plan on extending your field of observations, think about lightweight glasses of a convenient size. Thirty ounces, or forty ounces does not seem like much—and when you try them on in the shop they seem light. But after an hour's walking, forty ounces seems much, much heavier and weight increases with every extra foot you walk.

It is nice to be able to buy new glasses. But it is not necessary. New glasses for a beginning bird watcher may be too costly. Or as in our case, one pair of glasses may not be sufficient for the family. Some birds will not sit in the same place long enough to pass the glasses around. At any rate, there are many reputable dealers of used glasses. Most times you get a new glass guarantee—and well-made glasses are good for a lifetime. *Audubon Magazine,* 1000 Fifth Avenue, New York, N. Y. frequently carries the advertising of some very reputable dealers in New York and elsewhere, specializing in glasses for bird watching.

Bird Watching Around the Year

One interesting feature of bird watching around the year is that each season brings a change—a change in the birds you see, and a change in their activities. Consequently, the changing seasons and birds provide different phases of your bird hobby.

By and large birds fall into five groups, classified according to the season of the year in your area. It will require considerable observation to place all birds in their correct groupings because there is some overlapping. But this is one of the interesting things about bird watching—the possibility of seeing a bird out of season, when by all the bird books it ought to be in Central or South America. On the other hand, you will soon be able to explode many a myth about an early winter—or an early spring—based on birds being seen out of season.

For many years newspapers have heralded the arrival of the first robins as big news—any time from February to March. Spring is just around the corner. But for several years we have seen robins—as many as forty—during Christmas week.

A sure sign of winter is supposed to be the arrival of geese on their way south. But when you keep bird records for several years, you will find the geese vary only a few days one year from the next, and cold weather sets in early or late—regardless of geese. It is interesting to check your observations against some of these age-old folk stories.

The first group of birds to get to know are those which live permanently in your area. These birds are called permanent residents. Birds such as crows, song sparrows, chickadees, downy woodpeckers, and blue jays frequently live the year round in a relatively small area. They may travel quite a distance to feed but many of them spend their lives within an area of a few square miles.

Of course, it is difficult to tell whether the particular jay, downies or chickadees are the same ones you saw during the summer. Perhaps the birds you saw then migrated southward during the fall, and similar birds from up north some place migrated south from there to winter in your area.

At any rate, in most places, there is a group of birds that remains more or less constant throughout the year, and you can get to know them easily, since you may see them so often. On top of that, with the exception of crows, these are the birds that most readily visit feeding stations, bird baths and dusting areas in the yard.

Even while living in a city apartment we have had three birds visit a window feeder the year round—English sparrows, starlings, and blue jays. They were not the most desirable birds perhaps, in the eyes of many people, but they did provide plenty of entertainment for our young daughter.

The second group that is easy to learn is made up of those birds which are summer residents. These are birds that spend the winter to the south—sometimes not too far from where you live. But in the spring, they migrate to your area, mate, nest and raise their young. Orioles, some of the warblers, swallows, cuckoos, thrashers and some of the thrushes are examples of birds that are typical summer residents. Of course, there are many more, but not too many of them will nest in or near the yard where you can enjoy them without short hikes into woods and fields.

This group of birds is one of the most interesting if you are fortunate enough to have them select your garden or a neighboring yard or park for a nesting site. While they are nesting and raising their young, birds are usually quiet and as unobtrusive as possible. But you can feel fairly certain that most birds visiting your bird bath or hopping about the lawn or in the shrubbery during late May and June are nesting not too far away. The next job is to find the nest, and this is much more difficult than it sounds.

A pair of song sparrows nested in a rambler rose not six feet from our dining-room windows, and it was not until the young were large enough to fly that we discovered the nest.

Only when we started to spray the bush to try to kill the aphis that infested it did we see the startled adults fly out. Investigation showed three well-grown young about ready to fly.

Robins selected a blue spruce about five feet from the house, and a point not more than eight feet from our bedroom window for a nesting site. But so quiet were they that we failed to see it until a mid-May storm blew one of the young birds out of the nest. We found it on the front steps, thoroughly soaked and apparently half-dead. As we stooped to pick it up, we heard the alarm note of the adult overhead, and looked up to see the nest. We placed the young bird back where it belonged and, as far as we know, it recovered completely from its dousing. Since then, we have watched regularly and each year have found robins nesting in or near the same place.

Several years ago we fell heir to a young sparrow hawk that was hatched and spent three or four weeks as a nestling in the raingutter of a fashionable New York apartment in the East Sixties, within a few feet of the bed of some friends. They were totally unaware of the birds—male, female, and two young—until the young were learning to fly. Then one of the young, testing its new-found flying ability, wound up on the bureau in the bedroom. The noise of one of the adults trying to get the bird to fly back out of the open window awoke the slumbering humans who promptly slammed the window and put a huge hatbox over the harmless hawk. Thus we had a sparrow hawk on our hands, for which we arose an hour early every day to scamper through the meadow chasing grasshoppers, beetles and other large and fleshy insects to satisfy the seemingly insatiable appetite of a young and healthy hawk. Ground meat and gristle supplied some of its food, but its preference was a nice, fat grasshopper—and those insects are few and far between in June on suburban Long Island. How happy we were when the bird was old enough to fly and feed itself.

But if you find a nest you have many interesting hours in store for you. While the birds are incubating the eggs there is not much to see. But when the eggs hatch, the fun starts. For the adults form a seemingly never-ending chain gang bringing food, filling hungry offspring, only to fly away for more food. If feeding your own offspring at four-hour intervals seemed a difficult routine, count the number of times an adult robin feeds its young in a two-hour period.

As the young grow large enough to leave the nest more fun awaits. For even after the young can fly, they still must be fed for a few days by the never-tiring adults. And every time we see a full-grown bird being fed, we cannot help but remember a poem by Dr. Eugene Edmund Murphey, "Catbird Wisdom."

> . . . . Yesterday, fully grown, competent,
> One of the young came, fluttering
> Wings aquiver, begging his Father
> For worms.
> If I had bred a hulking son
> Who came to me, shivering and whining
> For money—That essential worm of humanity—
> I hope I'd have the wisdom of the catbird
> To give him hell
> And run him off the place.*

* From *Wings at Dusk* by Eugene Edmund Murphey
Longmans, Green and Co., Inc., New York, 1939.

The third group of birds, and also easy to get to know, is that which spends the winter in the neighborhood of your home. These birds probably nest to the north, but in some cases they may not nest too far away. Such typical back yard birds as tree sparrows, white-throated sparrows, purple finches and juncos nest to the north of us, but spend the winter feeding at our window and garden feeders.

They begin to arrive in November or December, and depending upon the severity of the winter, become regular or sporadic visitors.

A heavy snow or sleet will usually bring them flocking to the yard where they become quite tame and easily observed. All it takes is a well- and frequently-stocked feeder to attract them and on those blustery winter afternoons when it is much nicer indoors than out, these birds can provide a great deal of interest.

Many bird observers have found some unusual birds feeding in their yards. One friend of ours has seen an Oregon junco in his Long Island garden—not unusual in Oregon or California, but most unusual on the East Coast.

So interested have several of our friends become in the back yard birding, that a sort of rivalry has sprung up as to which of us can attract the most unusual or interesting birds. It is quite common now for the phone to ring anytime from dawn to dusk on a winter Sunday, and to hear a coy voice ask, "Guess what we've got?" Of course, we cannot guess, and when told, we usually jump into the car and tear over to see it. Sometimes the bird has long since departed for other places. But usually, they stay long enough for a quick look. It is surprising how easily you can scare up an impromptu cocktail party or buffet supper this way. For once the clan gathers on a Sunday afternoon, and stories about "what we had today" start, time means nothing. The unfortunate host who has had the rarity finds he has a party on his hands. After all, he can't go out and cook up his own light supper. And what can you do about those talkative birders? It would be a mean trick not to ask them over to see the bird—but why can't they go home? Well, maybe someone else will get stuck next week.

Last winter we discovered two owls in a pine grove next to our home, a long-eared owl which is quite common in our area, and a saw whet which is rather unusual—it was that year anyway.

We felt sure that the birds would stay there, so we ate a leisurely dinner and got busy on the phone. In an hour or two those owls in that small grove had lost all their privacy. Some ten people were stalking through the woods, binoculars on the alert, watching for either or both of the birds. But only the long-ear was there. The saw whet was gone. But was he? What was that on the ground? Ten birders gathered in a circle and examined a handful of feathers. It certainly looked like the remains of the tiny saw whet. Perhaps the saw whet was still there, but invisible to our eyes. It certainly appeared that the long-ear had eaten the smaller owl. Could he? We think so, even if we could not prove it.

The fourth group of birds, and probably the largest, consists of those birds that stop in for a while as they migrate north in the spring, or south in the later summer or fall. Warblers, thrushes, grosbeaks, some of the hawks, and some of the sparrows are typical examples of birds that you can

watch for only a few days before they move north to nest
or south to spend the winter.

It is during these migration periods that you realize what
a large number of birds there are—and how such things can
happen as the large number of warblers and vireos that are
killed by flying into New York's Empire State Building on
fall nights.

For as you look around your garden one day the birds are
the usual permanent residents. Then after a few warm spring
days and nights, suddenly one morning the garden is swarm-
ing with birds. Warblers flit about the new-formed leaves;
four or five scarlet tanagers appear in the apple tree; and half
a dozen orioles sing from the highest points. Over in the
fence row, a chewink repeatedly calls the sound which gave
it its name, and the first catbird announces its arrival.

Warblers especially arrive in waves—large numbers one
day, building up to a peak a day or so later; then dying out
to a very few. Again, a week or so later perhaps, another
wave arrives to spend a day or so. For these birds fly at night,
and stop during the day to feed and to rest. Early morning
is the time to see them at their best. For some reason, the
early morning light and the dew still on the leaves, seem to
intensify the already brilliant colors of the redstart, magnolia,
blackburnian, parula, and Canada warblers. Perhaps it is just
the peace and quiet of the garden at seven or eight o'clock,
when neighbors have not yet begun to whistle for their dogs
and the air is not filled with the shouts of future big league
ball players, but the combination of colorful songs and brilliant plumage against the delicate blossoms of apple and
pear is one of our favorites. Birding the rest of the year is

fun. But nothing can compare with the first wave of spring migrants.

The last groups of birds are those casual visitors in winter or summer. These birds nest either far to the north or to the south, and have a more or less definite area where they spend the winter or summer. But in between times they wander around and end up for a few days near your home. The Oregon junco mentioned before is an example. A magpie, which one winter spent several weeks just outside New York City, is another example.

In general, the birds in this group vary in numbers and you can never be sure of seeing them. Some years they turn up—some years they do not. But they fall in a category different from the first four groups because there is nothing regular about their habits.

Bird Hobbies

We realize very well that a hobby means something different to each individual interested in it. Some folks will ride it for all it is worth, while others will take it or leave it. But based on our experience over some dozen years, we have a few suggestions to those who really want to have fun watching birds—and this applies especially to those with youngsters in the family.

Do not ever be satisfied with just looking at birds and exclaiming, "Oh, aren't they cute." Yes, they may be cute, depending upon how you look at them, but there is much more to it than that. Birds are so interesting that many people have spent their lives studying them—many more spend almost all of their free time studying them. And there are

a great many aspects to bird study. We do not suggest that
everyone become an ornithologist in the strict sense of the
word. But anyone who confines his interest just to looking
at birds soon loses interest and wonders what there is to get
excited about in bird watching. Our answer to this question
is "nothing." Just watching is not very exciting for any long
period of time.

But if you keep records of what you see, you have the
basis of an interesting aspect of birding. Suppose the minute
you decide to pay a little more attention to the birds that
are flying around the yard, you start to keep a simple notebook. Under date entries, you list the birds you see. Jot
down a note or two on the weather—temperature, wind
direction, rain or snow, etc. After a while you will see that
birds come and go, building up to peaks at different times of
the year and dropping off at other times.

You may find, as we have, that wind direction has much
to do with whether or not you see birds, even more so than
temperature or other factors. You will have a record over a
year or more that later on will show you when you can expect to see certain birds. You can correlate the arrival of
certain birds with the weather—or show that weather does
not have much to do with it. More will be said later about
the mechanics of record keeping.

Another thing to notice is that most birds are usually associated with definite kinds of natural surroundings. For
example, tree sparrows which spend a large part of the winter in the northern part of the United States, are usually seen
in fields or hopping across the lawn. Rarely are they seen in
dense shrubbery. On the other hand, cardinals are usually

associated with thickets or densely-grown places. They may fly out to a feeder, but their usual haunt is where the foliage is thick.

Towhees, too, are usually seen in dense areas on the ground, scratching for grubs under the leaf mold. Orioles, on the other hand, are tree-top birds, coming down to water but usually seen high in an elm or oak.

Most birds have definite surroundings and even altitudes which they prefer. Some you see mostly on the ground; others halfway up a tree; still others near the top. Watch for these characteristics, because they help you identify the bird the next time you see it, and also help you to understand what the birds are doing.

Keeping records on nesting birds is another interesting aspect of bird watching. Note when the birds first start collecting bits of straw, string, and other nesting material, watch where they fly and find where they are building the nest. Then see how long it takes before they lay the first egg, the second and the third. Count the days that the eggs are incubated, and note when the young hatch. Then find out how long it takes before the young can live on their own.

Many other ideas of what to watch for will be given in later pages. But if you want to have the most fun out of bird watching, try to go beyond mere identification. That is fun for a while, but for most people it does not have lasting interest.

If you cannot do anything else, get a good book, besides the field guide, that will tell something about the birds you see. It is surprising how much geography, history and other things you can teach your youngsters by finding out where birds migrate to as they go north or south when they leave your yard. Some birds may stop in the southern United States, while others go on to Central America and South America. The tree sparrows and snow buntings you see in winter may nest as far north as the Arctic Circle. Think of all the territory they fly over to get to your yard, or to get to their nesting site from your yard. Migration routes can be traced on maps of North and South America, and your youngsters can get a vivid picture of the Western Hemisphere just by being interested in birds.

Perhaps after reading about birds you may find that your experiences over a few years differ from the observations of the author. Perhaps you will discover something about a particular bird that is relatively unknown to other bird watchers.

If you spend your vacations away from home, in the mountains, at the seashore, in the country, you can take your hobby along with you. With your glasses around your neck and your guide in your pocket, you are ready for more interesting experiences wherever you go. You may see new birds you cannot see at home, or you may see the same birds doing different things.

We had watched flickers, bluebirds, phoebes, ovenbirds, towhees and warblers in our suburban yard. But while on vacation at our favorite spot in the mountains we can watch these same birds nesting.

Related Hobbies

Becoming interested in birds is often the beginning of related hobbies. If you are already a photographer, you may get interested in making still or motion pictures of the birds that feed, nest, bathe, or just hop around your garden. If you are a gardener, you may develop an interest in planting certain shrubs and trees that have proved to be attractive to birds. Some flowers are quite attractive to hummingbirds, and other flowers when they go to seed, provide food for finches and other seed-eaters. More about these aspects in later chapters.

If you are a stamp collector, you can find a tremendously interesting hobby in looking for stamps that picture birds. Recently, the United States printed its first bird stamp, commemorating the establishment of the Everglades National Park. Some of the Central American and South American countries have long recognized the beauty of their native birds and have used them on stamps.

Perhaps your interest runs toward collecting prints, etchings, or paintings. There are many beautiful works of art on the market, from inexpensive reproductions to original oils that are appreciated all the more when you know the bird subjects in real life. When you know birds you can soon tell the difference between the artist who paints a bird in a studio and the artist who, after long hours of observation from a blind, paints a black duck jumping.

There are many other hobbies, new aspects of which will be open to you, if you get interested in birds. They will be all the more interesting if you know more about birds than just what they look like.

So, a bird hobby can be as interesting as you want to make it. You can watch the birds that happen to stop in your yard, or you can do everything possible to attract more birds to your garden. There are several ways of doing it, each successful at a different season of the year. Birdhouses in some places are very successful. Feeders and bird baths attract birds in most places. But planting certain plants that provide food and shelter seems to be the most practical way of all. Not long ago, we heard of a 20' x 40' yard in a densely-settled town that was a veritable sanctuary. Naturally, the owner was interested in birds. His yard was almost a jungle. But birds stopped there, more than a hundred species a year. He provided food and water but natural food and cover seem to do the trick.

Other chapters in this book will suggest ways of making your garden or yard a miniature bird sanctuary—for almost any yard, whether in city, suburbs or country, can be made to attract birds. For apartment house dwellers, there are usually near-by parks, and these are not to be overlooked by the city birder. One hundred and thirty-nine species of birds were observed in Central Park, New York in one year by a group of bird hobbyists. Forty-four species were found to visit a small New York City garden in one year. Our casual observations in our own suburban garden have turned up more than a hundred birds in or over the garden in a single year.

Size and location are both important, and both have a bearing on how many and what birds may be seen. But regardless of the size, some birds can be attracted and you can have fun watching them.

So let us look at how you can get birds to come to you, instead of your having to go to them. But first, let us look at some of the birds you may reasonably expect to see.

CHAPTER 2

WHAT BIRD IS THAT?

To THE newcomer to birding, the idea of learning a couple of hundred different kinds of birds seems like an insurmountable task. But it is not anywhere near as difficult as it sounds if you go about it in the right way.

First of all, starting out in the yard or garden has a distinct advantage. Usually, birds that appear at feeders, bird boxes or bird baths, or those which feed or take shelter in the shrubbery of the yard, come one or two species at a time. Rarely will there be a wave of many different species at any one time. In the course of a year it may be possible to see a hundred or more. But during any one day there will probably be only a few. Thus it is possible to learn one or two different birds a day or two dozen or so a week.

Secondly, the birds in the yard usually will be feeding, nesting or resting and will stay put long enough for careful observation. Some birds may be jumpy or wary, but most of them should be reasonably easy to watch. It goes without saying that the family cat should be kept indoors when you want to watch birds. Few things will clear the yard of birds as fast as tabby on the prowl.

Two things are important for successful observation. Get as close to the bird as you can without frightening it. This means that you must move slowly and not make any quick or sudden movements. Usually, you can tell whether the bird is frightened and about to fly. It becomes alert and wary. It looks around and may watch you closely. That is the time to stop and look. But if the bird continues to feed, preen its feathers, or perch with its feathers ruffled up and its head down low, then slowly walk closer, one step at a time.

The second thing that will make bird identification easier is to have the sun at your back, or at a thirty degree side-angle. It takes bright, direct sunlight to bring out the delicate colors in all their brilliance, and to make it possible for you to see some of the less obvious markings. Otherwise, you get only a silhouette, or at best see the bird as a drab brown, dull yellow, or faded blue. Frequently you may have to circle a tree or shrub to get the desired light, but the beauty of the coloring on many birds can only be appreciated when the sun shines directly on them.

In the beginning, as you first become acquainted with the birds in your yard or garden, do not be too concerned with individual species. Try instead to associate some general characteristics with the bird that will enable you to place it in the correct family—sparrow, warbler, flycatcher, thrush or woodpecker, for example. You will soon see that most warblers are found high in trees, flitting about the new-forming leaves as they search for insects. Some will search over each leaf. Others will dart around quickly among the leaves, and dart

out to catch an insect on the wing. Flycatchers will be seen
to perch on the end of a branch, and suddenly fly out several
feet after an insect. They will twist and turn as they follow
the bug through the air, and once they capture it, will return
to a perch to wait for another insect to fly by. Woodpeckers
are usually seen on the side of the trunk of a tree, or walking
along the branches, probing in the bark with their chisel-like
bills. When clinging to the side of the trunk, their stiff tail
acts as a support.

The flight characteristics of birds will help you place them
in the right family, whether or not you can see any coloring
or markings that will enable you to identify them according
to species. Woodpeckers, for example, generally have an un-
dulating flight, flying up and down as if they were flying
over rolling hills and shallow valleys. Finches have the same
sort of flight, but their ups and downs are closer together,
as if the hills and valleys were closer to each other.

Generally, most of the species within a family have similar
characteristics that, once you get to know them, will help you
place them immediately in the correct family. After that it is a
matter of tracing down individual characteristics, coloring,
markings or songs until the species is arrived at. Of course,
there are exceptions, as there are to any general rule. But that
is one more thing that makes bird watching interesting.

In the long run, bird identification is largely a process of
elimination. By noting actions, profile or flight characteristics,
general habits, and the place where you see the bird, you can
tell almost at once what the bird is not. Almost instantly, you
can place it in one or two possible families. Where you see it
—on the ground, in a tree, in dense shrubbery, in the open;

when you see it—the season of the year; and what it is doing, usually helps eliminate all but a few possible varieties. Then, a knowledge of individual habits, markings and color will help you track down the bird.

For example, you can tell a sparrow hawk a half-mile away by the way it flutters and hovers over an open field; or a meadowlark by its fluttery flight; or you can almost always spot a towhee just by the sound of the dead leaves being kicked around in a thicket as the bird searches for grubs and bugs.

Knowing bird songs is also a great aid to identification as well as one of the genuine pleasures of birding. If you start learning call notes and songs as you learn birds, it is not a particularly difficult job. Start with the common birds around the yard and build up to the migrants that you see only once a year. Before long you will be able to pick out a red-eyed vireo or parula warbler just by the call or song coming from the cherry tree or dogwood.

It is far beyond the scope of this book to describe in detail all the birds that might be seen in any yard or garden in the country at any time of year. That job would fill a volume far larger than this and call for an author far more experienced than this one. The purpose of this chapter is to describe briefly some of the more common birds that may be seen in different parts of the country. This chapter is planned as no more than a suggested list of what may be found, showing briefly when birds are seen and their usual habits in the yard.

An added problem is the fact that a bird may be classified as an eastern bird and yet never turn up in a yard in New Jersey, Connecticut or Virginia. Tufted titmice, as an example, are common just west of the Hudson River, but rarely are recorded on Long Island. Cardinals turn up regularly in gardens on the north shore of Long Island, but much less commonly on the south shore, scarcely fifteen miles away. The exact location of the yard in relation to individual bird flyways, natural habitat preferences and the altitude, all have a bearing on which birds will be seen.

That is an added reason for getting to know bird families first. Then use the previously mentioned bird guides to track down the species.

The illustrations following page 52 are also planned to show only some of the more common birds of the yard or garden in their characteristic poses. They will serve, too, as identification aids for a few species in each of the several families portrayed.

The following list of birds has been organized in a way that is thought to be the easiest to use for newcomers to the hobby of bird watching. Families are listed alphabetically, and common representatives of each family are listed alphabetically within the family. In cases where the family to which a bird belongs is not obvious, the common name is in its alphabetical arrangement, with a cross-reference to the family.

In reading this list of bird descriptions it will be seen that certain size comparisons are used. English sparrows and robins are used for comparison since they are reasonably well known by most people, or very easily learned. Thus birds are said to be larger or smaller than a sparrow, or larger or smaller than a robin. This provides a close enough idea of relative size to make identification possible. Most bird books give the length of a bird in inches, which for advanced bird watchers is excellent. But this observer never has succeeded in having a warbler stand still long enough for him to use a ruler and decide whether the length might be four and one-half or five and one-half inches. Even with good binoculars sizes based on metric measurements are difficult to estimate when a bird is in flight or perched in the top of an oak. Relative size is important, but exact size is a difficult thing to determine.

BLACKBIRD FAMILY

Bobolink—Larger than a sparrow. Black below and white above. Females and males in the fall, and young are buff colored with dark stripes on head and upper parts. Nests in open fields and is frequently seen perching on a fence or rail singing the song that gives it its name.

Cowbird—Smaller than a robin. Male, bluish-black bird with brown head and heavy, sparrow-like bill. Female, mouse-gray all over. Readily visits feeders and bird baths the year round north at least to southern New England. Does not build its own nest, but habitually lays eggs in other birds' nests, leaving them to be hatched by the "foster parent."

Grackle, Purple—Larger than a robin, purplish black, long tail. Bright white eye in spring is easily visible as bird feeds on lawn or bathes in bird bath. Nests occasionally on edges of gardens or yard in trees, frequently in conifers. May visit feeders the year round south of New York.

Meadowlark, Eastern—About robin size. Brownish above, yellow below, with black crescent-patch on breast.

Short tail with white feathers on outer edges. Nests in fields, and is usually•seen fluttering over a meadow or singing from a fencepost. Occasionally winters in northern U. S.

Meadowlark, Western—Similar to Eastern in size and appearance. Song is very different, being richer and more ringing. Song has seven or more notes, gurgling and more pleasant than the Eastern bird.

Oriole, Baltimore—Smaller than a robin. Male, bright orange and black. Females, greenish yellow above, yellowish underneath. Two white wing bars. Song is an easy-to-recognize series of piping notes. Nests in the tops of high trees, usually elms in towns or villages, in a basket-like, hanging nest. Will visit bird baths, and will collect nesting material in the yard.

Oriole, Orchard—Smaller than a robin. Male, black head, neck, back, wings and tail. Belly a deep chestnut color. Female, greenish above, yellowish below, with two white bars on wings.

Oriole, Bullock's—Western version of Baltimore Oriole. Smaller than robin. Male, bright orange and black, with prominent white wing patches. Females grayish green above, yellowish white below. Only oriole found in most parts of western U. S. Nests high in trees, in bag-like nest, hanging from branch.

Red-wing—Slightly smaller than a robin. Male is black with red patches at bend of wings. Red may not show if bird is perching, but a buffy stripe may be seen. Female, a brownish, heavily-striped bird with a marked buffy streak over eye. Nests in swampy places, but will visit feeders in winter or early spring.

BLUEBIRD see Thrushes

BOBOLINK see Blackbirds

BOBWHITE see Quail

BUNTINGS see Sparrows and Finches

CARDINAL see Sparrows and Finches

CATBIRD see Mockingbird

CHAT see Warblers

CHICKADEES see Titmice

COWBIRD see Blackbirds

CREEPER see Nuthatches and Creepers

CROSSBILLS see Sparrows and Finches

CUCKOO

Cuckoo, Black-billed—Larger than a robin. Brown above, white underneath. Black bill. If these birds nest in the vines or bushes on the edge of the garden you will know it—for they frequently sing at night. The call is characteristic cu cu cu cu cu cu cu cu cu in rapid succession.

Cuckoo, Yellow-billed—Larger than a robin. Slim in appearance. Long tail. Dull brown above and white underneath. White spots at tip of tail. Yellow lower mandible. Reddish tinge in wings is distinguishing mark when in flight. Nests in thicket or low bush and noted as destroyer of tent caterpillars.

DICKCISSEL see Sparrows and Finches

DOVE

> *Dove, Mourning*—Larger than a robin. A brown pigeon, smaller than domestic pigeon. Has a pointed tail which flashes white spots when the bird flies. Wings make a whistling noise when bird flies. Usually seen in garden pecking at new shoots, or on lawn eating seeds. Characteristically perches on wires or fence. Call is a typical pigeon—coo coo coo.

FINCHES see Sparrows and Finches

FLICKER see Woodpeckers

FLYCATCHERS

> *Phoebe*—Sparrow sized flycatcher, grayish above and white below. Persistent tail wagger as it perches. May nest under eaves of house or out-building, or under a bridge. Typically a flycatcher in actions. Song, fee-bee, fee-bee, the "bee" being first higher then lower than first syllable. One of first birds to arrive in spring.
> *Wood Peewee*—Sparrow size. Olive brown on top, whitish below, with two wing bars. This is a flycatcher, and has typical flycatcher habits. Nests in trees on top of limb, and may nest in orchard or grove.
> *Kingbird, Eastern*—Smaller than a robin. A large flycatcher, dark gray above with black crown and tail. White underneath. White band on tip of tail. Flies from

one perch to another in search of insects and frequently takes off after a flying hawk or crow to drive it away. Nests in trees, occasionally near buildings.

Kingbird, Western—Smaller than a robin. Grayish head and back, yellowish underneath. Sides of black, tail, white, instead of tip as in Eastern Kingbird. Typically a flycatcher in action. Nests around houses in western U. S., sometimes in birdhouses. Seen occasionally in east in fall.

Flycatcher, Least—Smaller than a sparrow. Dark above and light underneath. Noticeable white eyering, and two white wing bars. Nests on edges of woods, in orchards and around farms. Call is a distinctive che-bek with the accent on the *bek*. Like most flycatchers it perches on a branch, and then darts out for an insect, returning to its perch.

Flycatcher, Crested—Smaller than a robin. Reddish tail, gray breast and yellow belly. Greenish-gray on back. Sometimes nests in birdhouses, if houses are placed in woods which the bird prefers.

Flycatcher, Olive-sided—About sparrow size. Greenish brown above and whitish underneath. Two white wing bars. Nests in conifers and is seen usually during migration, as it visits the garden to feed on insects. Usually perches on end of branch to dart out after an insect, then returns to perch to wait for another bug.

GOATSUCKERS

Whip-Poor-Will—If a whip-poor-will nests nearby, there is little doubt about it. For its loud whip-poor-will call is repeated endlessly from dusk to dawn and announces its presence. Brownish bird with white tail feathers on male.

Nighthawk—Robin sized, slender winged relative of the whip-poor-will. White patches on wings. Dark brown in color. Flies over towns and cities at dusk, darting after insects. Seen during day in migration. Sometimes nests on flat, gravel roofs, right on stones. Call resembles that of unhappy Dodger fan razzing the umpire.

GRACKLE see Blackbirds

HAWKS

At first we were doubtful of the wisdom of listing these three hawks as birds seen in the yard or garden, because usually, when they are seen, it is as they prey on smaller birds. This natural habit of getting food where it is easiest to find it makes many people rather unhappy—so unhappy in fact that they take steps to eliminate the hawks. We thought it best, at first, not to draw attention to the hawks' feeding habits.

But on second thought we realized that here was an opportunity to say a word in favor of hawks. First of all, hawks are wild birds and as such have as much a place in nature as a junco or flicker. It is as natural for them to feed on birds as it is for juncos to eat weed seeds, or flickers to eat insects.

To a large extent, the birds eaten by hawks are the less healthy individuals. Thus by destroying them, hawks may be protecting other birds by cutting off the source of disease.

In most gardens, hawks will catch the easiest prey—and

this is usually the English sparrow or starling, which are less accustomed to dodging hawks. All three of these hawks have spent considerable time in our yard, and we have watched them catch birds. In every case but two, the less desirable species were the prey. A tree sparrow and a catbird were the two that we would have preferred to see unharmed— but to a sincerely interested bird watcher, the thrill of seeing the hawks far overcame any antipathy to birds killed.

Last but not least, hawks have been eating birds for many, many years—far more years than man has been here to "protect" song birds by predatory control. There is no indication that any bird population has been threatened by hawks. For hawks are one of nature's balancers, and the food they take helps keep the scales balanced.

Hawk, Cooper's—Smaller than a crow. Short winged, long tailed. Bluish-gray back, brownish streaked breasts. May be seen perched in tree, watching feeder or bird bath, waiting the chance to snatch a meal of a songbird. Most common in gardens in winter.

Hawk, Sharp-shinned—Larger than a robin. Short, round wings, long tail. Bluish-gray back, brownish breast. Like the Cooper's, this hawk may rarely feed on birds in the garden.

Hawk, Sparrow—A robin size hawk, with reddish tail, blue-gray wings and a black and white face. It hovers frequently in one spot as it searches for food. Frequently seen on poles or wires. Feeds usually on large insects or mice, occasionally on small birds in the garden. Nests in holes in trees, occasionally in birdhouses.

HUMMINGBIRDS

Hummingbird, Black-chinned—Hummingbirds are the smallest of all birds. Wings move so quickly that they are only a blur. Almost bumblebee-like in action. Long needle-like bill for probing flowers. The black-chinned hummingbird is a common western species known for its black throat and white patch below it. Greenish on top. Female, greenish above, white below. Seen in garden, darting among flowers in search of honey.

Hummingbird, Ruby-throated—Only hummingbird seen in East. Greenish above, with red throat. Females have whitish throat. Visits gardens and may be attracted by sugar-water solution in brightly colored tubes, tied to garden plants. Will also drink at bird baths.

Hummingbird, Rufous—Small hummingbird, bright reddish brown on top. Throat bright red. Female, greenish-bronze on top, white below. Seen usually in migration as it visits garden flowers to feed.

JAY

Jay, Blue—Larger than a robin. Bright blue on top, whitish below, and with a crest. Readily recognized by a harsh call. Common garden visitor and may nest in shrubs or trees at edge of garden. Will defend nest by flying and pecking at intruder. Year round resident in many sections of country.

JUNCO see Sparrows

KINGBIRD see Flycatcher

KINGLETS

Kinglet, Golden-crowned—Much smaller than a sparrow, even smaller than warblers. Greenish-gray back, white below. Bright orange crown in male, yellow in female. White stripe over eye. Usually seen in evergreens.

Kinglet, Ruby-crowned—A very small bird, greenish-gray above, white below, with a reddish crown. Short tail, two wing bars. Partial white eyering. Seen during migration or in winter.

MOCKINGBIRD, THRASHERS, CATBIRD

Catbird—Smaller and more streamlined than robin. Grayish in color with black cap on head. Mewing call, from which it gets its name, is distinctive. Nests in thickets and dense shrubs. May visit garden the year round, being attracted to feeder in winter and bird bath in summer.

Mockingbird—Robin size, but slimmer and with longer tail. Gray above, white underneath. White patches on wings and tail. Nests in trees or bushes in towns and rural areas from Maryland to Nebraska south (Western Mockingbird, from Central California east and south). Occasionally seen north in late summer and fall.

Thrasher, Brown—Larger than a robin, but slimmer, reddish brown, and with a long tail. Heavily streaked breast. Curved bill. Has a distinctive song. Nests in thickets and dense bushes, and may nest at edge of garden. Visits bird bath and feeders in fall and spring.

NIGHTHAWK see Goatsuckers

NUTHATCHES AND CREEPER

> *Nuthatch, Red-breasted*—Smaller than sparrow. Grayish above, black crown, white line over eye. Reddish-buff underneath. Nests in hollow trees or in birdhouses. May visit suet feeders, or suet stuck in bark of trees. Seen usually in winter in northern half of U. S.
>
> *Nuthatch, White-breasted*—Smaller than sparrow. Slate gray above, white below. Known as "upside down" bird for its habit of hanging on tree or suet rack with head down. Nests in hollow trees or bird boxes.
>
> *Creeper, Brown*—Smaller than sparrow. Slim, and brown all over. Thin, curved bill and a stiff tail that is used as a support in the manner of a woodpecker. Its interesting characteristic is that it climbs the tree spirally, then flits to the bottom of the next tree. Attracted by suet feeders.

ORIOLES see Blackbirds

OVENBIRD see Warblers

OWLS

> *Owl, Screech*—A small owl, robin sized, but more plump. Two colors—reddish or gray. Noticeable tufts on either side of head. Nests in holes in trees, rarely in birdhouses. Heard at night, voice being a mournful wail, running down the scale. If a screech owl is around, it may be attracted by "squeaking" like a mouse, or rubbing two flat sticks together so they squeak.
>
> *Owl, Saw Whet*—A very small owl, smaller than screech

owl, and without tufts. Brownish above, streaked below. Very tame, and can be approached quite close. Found in conifers during winter, or in other trees in sheltered spots. Nests in hollow trees.

PEWEE see Flycatchers

PHEASANT see Quail and Pheasant

PHOEBE see Flycatchers

PLOVER

Killdeer Plover—A robin size bird, grayish above, white below, and with two black bands across breast. May be seen running across lawn, ploughed field or pasture, probing for grubs and insects. If disturbed near nest, will fly in circles calling loudly "kill-dee, kill dee."

QUAIL AND PHEASANT

Bobwhite—Small chicken-like bird about the size of a robin. Male, reddish-brown with white throat and white stripe over eye. The female is duller. Recognized by clear whistle that gives it the name. Nests on ground in brush patches or along edges of fields.

Pheasant, Ring-necked—Large, chicken-like bird. Male brightly colored brown, with white collar, and long pointed tail. Female dull brownish, with shorter pointed tail. Introduced as game bird, and inhabits open country from which it wanders into gardens and yards to feed in fall and winter.

RED-WING see Blackbirds

ROBIN see Thrushes

SPARROWS AND FINCHES

Towhee—Smaller than a robin and more slender. Male, head and back black. Sides color of robin's breast. Belly white. White spots on tail visible in flight. Female, brown where male is black. Known also as chewink, because of call which resembles that sound. May nest in bushy place at edge of yard or garden and drink at bird bath.

Sparrow, White-throated—Medium size sparrow, with gray breast, distinctive white throat, and black and white stripes on head. Yellowish spot in front of eye. Song has been interpreted to resemble "Old Sam Peabody, Peabody, Peabody." Will be attracted to feeders in yard in fall, and may stay all winter.

Sparrow, Tree—Medium sized sparrow that is seen only in winter. Round black spot in middle of clear breast. Reddish brown cap on head. Two white wing bars. Will visit yard in winter to feed on seeds scattered on ground or snow. More common in open country and brush patches on edges of woods.

Sparrow, Vesper—Medium sized sparrow with distinctive outer white tail feathers noticeable when bird flies. Breast lightly streaked. Will come to garden or yard during migration and occasionally in winter.

Sparrow, White-crowned—Medium large sized sparrow with clear gray breast and high, rounded head with black and white stripes. Pinkish bill. Chiefly a bird of central west, but may be seen occasionally in east during migration in spring or fall.

Sparrow, Field—Medium size sparrow with pink bill. Clear breast, and reddish brown on top. Nests in brushy places and edges of clearings. Visits gardens during migration and in winter will be attracted by feeders.

Sparrow, Fox—A large sparrow with a bright reddish tail. Heavily striped breast. Brown back. Nests in woods and thickets, but will be attracted in winter and fall to feeders in garden or yard. A planting of conifers may shelter one or two all winter.

Sparrow, Song—A medium sized sparrow, with streaked breast and a large spot in center of breast. Musical song familiar to most gardeners since the bird frequently nests in rambler roses or other tangles in garden or along edge.

Siskin, Pine—Smaller than sparrow. A finch, brownish and very streaked. Yellowish spots on wing and tail. Usually seen as the name implies, in conifers. Flying overhead, it resembles a goldfinch.

Sparrow, Chipping—Medium size sparrow. Streaked brown above, grayish below. Bright reddish cap on head, black line through eye. Nests in tree or bush. Will visit feeders during migration, and occasionally in winter.

Sparrow, English—Probably best known bird in the U. S. Male, brownish on top, gray underneath, gray crown and black throat. Female a dull brown, lighter underneath. Nests on buildings in eaves, vines, or even in birdhouses. Too common at winter feeders.

Redpoll, Common—A winter bird in northern U. S. Grayish brown, streaked birds, reddish on top of head. May visit feeders where they eat seeds.

Junco, Oregon—About sparrow size. Black head, red-brown back, sides yellowish or brownish, belly white. Normally found in west, but may turn up at feeders in east in winter.

Junco, Slate-colored—About sparrow size. Black head, gray back, white belly. White outer tail feathers. Pinkish bill. Usually seen in winter at feeding stations. Common junco of the East, seen occasionally west of the Rockies.

Grosbeak, Evening—Larger than a sparrow. Male, dullish yellow, with black wings with white patches. Female grayish, yellow· tinged, black and white wings. Bill whitish. Seen occasionally in winter, south to Missouri and New York, attracted to feeders.

Grosbeak, Rose-breasted—Larger than a sparrow. Male, black and white with large red patch on breast. Female, streaked yellowish brown with white wing bars. Large, conical bill. Song something like robin. Seen usually during migration as it stops in the garden to rest.

Goldfinch—Smaller than a sparrow. Male, yellow with black wings. Female, dull greenish—yellow with black wings and white wing bars. In winter male resembles female. Heavy bill identifies bird as a finch. Nests in trees on edges of fields. May visit feeder in winter, or bird bath in summer.

Finch, Purple—About sparrow size. Male a raspberry red with a heavy conical bill. Female, striped brown with a white line over eye. Nests in conifers south to Long Island, and in mountains to Maryland. Visits feeders and bird baths the year round from southern New England south.

Finch, House—About sparrow size. Brownish with red breast, forehead and rump. Female, a brownish striped bird sparrow-like in appearance. Dusky white underneath. A western bird (found also locally on Long Island). Nests about buildings in bushes or trees, sometimes atop buildings.

Dickcissel—About sparrow size, but slimmer. Male, brownish, yellow breast and black bib. Female, paler, tinge of yellow on breast, and lacking the bib. Midwestern bird of the open fields. Seen occasionally in the east at feeders.

Crossbill, White-winged—Sparrow size. Male, pinkish with black wings and tail and white wing bars. Female and young, greenish-gray with yellow rump and distinguished from red crossbill by two white wing bars. Like the red crossbill, feeds in conifers and is found usually in winter in northern U.S.

Crossbill, Red—About sparrow size. Male, red with dusky wings and tail. The cross-bill is an easy distinguishing mark. Female, dull greenish-gray with yellowish rump and underparts. Generally seen in winter in northern U.S. where it feeds on seeds in cones of evergreens.

Bunting, Eastern Painted—Smaller than sparrow and brightly colored. Male, bluish on head, green on back, red on rump and underparts. Female, greenish above and pale beneath. Nests in southern United States in brushy places, thickets and shrubs around gardens.

Cardinal—Slightly smaller than a robin. Male, all red except for black patch on face. Female, yellowish-brown with reddish showing. Red bill and crest make it unmistakable. Nests in thickets and dense shrubs around garden. Attracted to feeders by sunflower and other seeds.

Bunting, Indigo—Smaller than a sparrow. Male, blue all over, turning to brown in fall. Female, brown on top, paler brown beneath. Nests in brush patches, low in bushes or on ground.

STARLING

Starling—Smaller than a robin. A short-tailed blackbird, glossy purplish-green in spring, with a yellow bill. In fall and winter blackish with white speckles and dark bill. Nests in holes in trees, and may drive other birds from birdhouses. Feeds on suet and occasionally seeds. Destroys large numbers of grubs in lawns.

SWALLOWS AND SWIFT

Martin, Purple—Larger than a sparrow, this bird is the largest swallow. Male, bluish-black all over. Female, light below. Nests in birdhouses and around buildings. Usually nests in colonies. Recognized as a swallow by its habit of flying along, swooping and diving after insects.

Swallow, Barn—Slightly larger than sparrow, but with deep-forked tail. Dark blue on back, belly buff colored and throat and breast chestnut. One of family of birds characterized by long wings and a graceful flight. They swoop over meadows and ponds in search of insects and are seen most often on the wing. Nests in barns and buildings, making nests on rafters or beams.

Swallow, Cliff—Sparrow size. Blue on top, square tail.

Throat chestnut, other underparts light. Buff colored rump as it flies, a distinguishing mark. Nests on outside of barns, under eaves. Seen usually in flight searching for insects.

Swallow, Tree—Sparrow size. Blue-black or green-black above, depending upon light. White underneath. Nests usually near water, in hollow tree or birdhouse. Seen usually during fall migration as flocks fly around over the garden feeding as they move southward.

Swallow, Violet-green—A small swallow, dark greenish-purple above, white underneath. White patches on back just above tail. A western bird, nests on cliffs or in birdhouses.

Swift, Chimney—Slightly smaller than a sparrow, blackish and resembling a swallow somewhat in actions. Long, stiff wings and apparently without a tail. Chief characteristic in flight is the illusion that the wings beat alternately, for the bird tips from side to side as it flies. Nests in old chimneys around towns.

TANAGERS

Tanager, Scarlet—Slightly larger than a sparrow. Male brilliant scarlet with black wings and tail. Female, greenish above and yellowish below, with darker wings. Nests in woods or orchards, but visits bird bath and garden to feed. Song resembles a hoarse robin.

Tanager, Summer—Larger than a sparrow. Male, rosy-red all over. Female, greenish above, yellow underneath. Nests in woods, occasionally orchards north to Delaware and Wisconsin. Seen in garden as it feeds or drinks at bath.

Tanager, Western—Larger than a sparrow. Male, yellow with black wings. Red on front of head. Female, yellow below, and greenish above, with whitish wing bars. Found chiefly in western U. S., but has been recorded in east.

Titmouse, Chickadee

Titmouse, Tufted—About sparrow size. Gray colored, with buff or rust colored sides. Distinctive crest. Song is a distinctive "peter, peter, peter." Nests in holes in trees or in birdhouses. Will visit feeder in winter (from New Jersey south).

Chickadee, Black-capped—Smaller than sparrow. Black and white bird with black cap, white cheeks and a black bib. Nests in hole in trees, or in birdhouses. Visits feeders the year round within its range. The call for which it is named is easy to recognize.

Chickadee, Chestnut-backed—Smaller than a sparrow. Dark cap, white cheeks and dark bib are similar to black-capped chickadee, but the reddish back is different. Call somewhat harsher than black-cap. Found on Pacific Coast. Nests in birdhouses, and visits feeders.

Towhee see Sparrows

Thrasher see Mockingbird

Thrushes, Robin, Bluebird

Robin—Too well known to need much description. Gray back, rusty-red breast. Yellow bill. Will nest in garden, in conifers, fruit trees, or other trees providing good shelter. Feeds on lawn, and is frequent visitor at bird bath.

Thrush, Olive-backed—Larger than a sparrow. Gray-brown above, heavily spotted breast. No real distinctive markings. Buffy cheeks. Visits garden to feed or occasionally to use bird bath.

Thrush, Russet-backed—Larger than a sparrow. Found in western U. S., it has a grayish-brown back and heavily spotted breast. No distinctive markings. Buffy eyering may be noticeable.

Thrush, Varied—Robin size. Male, gray above, orange stripe through eye and orange bars on wing. Robin-colored breast with black band across it. Female, duller, with grayish band across breast.

Thrush, Wood—Smaller than a robin. Reddish head, brown back, and heavily spotted breast and sides. Song is beautiful as it rings from woods at dusk. May visit garden to use bird bath or to feed during migration.

Thrush, Gray-cheeked—Larger than a sparrow. Grayish brown above, white breast spotted with brown. As name implies, gray cheeks are distinctive. Seen usually during migration as it visits yard to use bird bath or feed.

Thrush, Hermit—Larger than a sparrow. Brown on back. Spotted breast. Rusty tail is distinguishing mark. Seen generally during migration, but may nest near garden in woodland. Song is one of most beautiful of bird songs. May winter as far north as southern New England and visit feeders during cold weather.

Bluebird, Eastern—About sparrow size. Male, bright blue above, reddish below. Female duller than male. Young are grayish with speckled breasts. Nests in hole in tree,

Warbler, Black-throated Gray—Smaller than a sparrow. A western warbler, gray back, white underneath, black and white face, and black throat. White wing bars. Female, duller, lacking black throat.

Warbler, Black-throated Green—Smaller than a sparrow. Male, greenish back, yellow on sides of head and neck. Black throat. Female, yellow patch on face, duller than male. Nests in evergreen woods, and usually seen in yard during spring migration. In breeding range may visit bird baths.

Warbler, Blackburnian—One of the more colorful warblers that is seen during migration in east. Male, black back, whitish underneath, with brilliant orange on throat, face and crown. Female, duller.

Warbler, Blue-winged—Medium sized warbler, yellowish underneath, darker back, black line through eye, grayish wings with two white wing bars. Common visitor in garden in breeding range, where it visits bird bath.

Warbler, Golden-winged—Medium sized warbler, blue-gray back, yellow patch on forehead, black throat, and white stripes on face. White underneath, yellow patch on wing. Female, duller. May nest near yard in east, and feed in trees around yard.

Warbler, Magnolia—Medium sized warbler, blackish on back, yellow underneath. Black stripes on breast, white patch on wings and sides of tail. Yellow throat contrast with gray head. Female, duller. Colorful bird that visits yard during migration.

Warbler, Myrtle—Medium sized warbler, bluish-gray back, white belly, yellow spot on crown, black across

PLATE 1

Upper left–white-throated sparrow   *Upper right*–song sparrow
Center right–chipping sparrow   *Lower right*–fox sparrow
Lower left–English sparrow

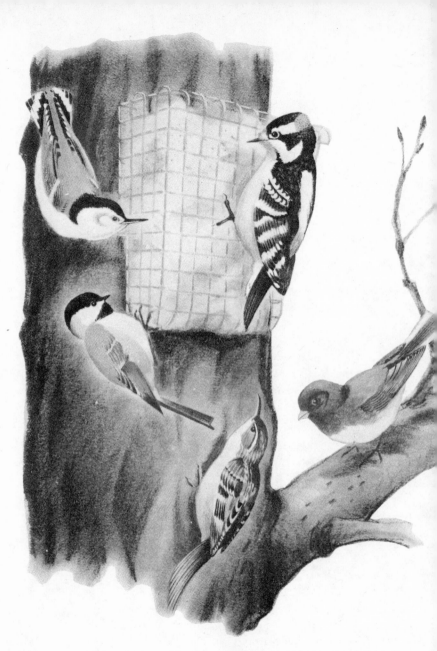

PLATE 2

Upper left—white-breasted nuthatch   *Upper right*—downy woodpecker
Lower right—slate-colored junco   *Lower center*—brown creeper
Center left—black-capped chickadee

PLATE 4

Top—mourning dove　　*Lower right*—flicker
Lower left—robin

Plate 5
Upper left—mockingbird   *Upper right*—catbird
Lower—brown thrasher

PLATE 6
Upper left–red-winged blackbird   *Center right*–blue jay
Lower left–Baltimore oriole

PLATE 7

Top–bluebird   *Center right*–cardinal
Lower–hermit thrush   *Center left*–house wren

PLATE 8
Upper left—chimney swift   *Upper right*—barn swallow
Lower right—purple martin

PLATE 9

Upper center—black and white warbler   *Upper right*—magnolia warbler
Center right—black-throated blue warbler *Lower*—redstart
Center left—myrtle warbler

PLATE 10

Upper left—western tanager   *Upper right*—western kingbird
Center—house finch   *Lower*—California thrasher
Center left—Bullock's oriole

PLATE 11
Top–cowbird   *Center*–starling
Lower–purple grackle

A blue jay visits the windowsill feeder for its favorite food, peanuts.

Chicadees are easily attracted to the yard or garden by suet or seeds.

The ever-present starling will eat almost anything, but prefers suet.

Three cowbirds visit a weathervane feeder to dine on milet, hemp, corn and sunflower seeds.

An unwelcome visitor at a bird feeder. It will eat more than a whole flock of birds.

wary catbird, up to his knees in water, looks e situation over.

A robin poses for a picture before taking a bath.

Besides adding color to the yard or garden, many flowering trees also attract birds. Dogwood provides food during fall and winter. Apple, pear and cherry serve a double use for man and bird.

ong sparrows frequently nest in rambler
ses or other such tangles around the yard.

Young song sparrows' insatiable appetites
mean the destruction of many garden grubs.

blue-winged warbler shakes and stretches
ter dunking in the bath.

An ovenbird rests for a moment on the edge
of the garden pool.

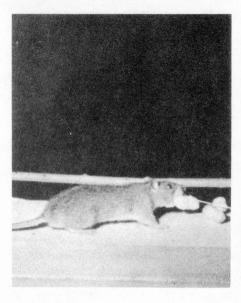

A nocturnal thief at the window bird feeder is "captured" by a camera trap.

Japanese beetles might cause more damage not controlled by some birds.

A wood thrush eyes the camera from a rock near the bird bath.

breast. Yellow rump and patch of yellow in front of each wing. Female, duller. Seen during spring migration, and in winter north to Massachusetts where it feeds on bay-berries and occasionally at feeders.

Warbler, Parula—Smallish warbler, bluish in color, yellow on throat and breast, dark band across the breast. Colorful little warbler with a distinctive song, seen generally during spring migration in yard as it feeds in trees.

Warbler, Palm—Medium sized warbler, brown on back, yellowish underneath, yellow line over eye. Distinctive rusty-red patch on head and whitish tinge on breast. Unlike most warblers, this species spends most of its time on ground. Among first of warblers to arrive in spring (Northeast) and occasionally winters in north where it turns up at feeders and winter bird baths.

Redstart—Medium sized warbler. Male, mostly black with white belly. Large patches of orange on sides of tail, front of wing and on wings. Female, quite different. Greenish-brown above, yellow patches on wings and tail, white underneath. Characterized by fluttering about in search of insects, chiefly in low trees and shrubs.

Warbler, Yellow—Medium size. Yellow all over, with reddish streaks on breast noticeable at close range. Females, duller. Nests around towns, usually in willows. One of first warbler arrivals.

Yellowthroat—Medium sized warbler. Gray-green on back, yellow throat and prominent black mask across face. Female, olive-brown with yellow throat and white underneath. Song a distinctive and easily learned "witch-ity, witchity, witchity." Nests in brushy patches on edges of marshes or swamps, occasionally near gardens if these conditions exist.

Ovenbird—About sparrow size, somewhat resembling a small thrush. Although a warbler, its habits are not typical of most warblers. Greenish-brown above, striped below. Orange patch on top of head. Heard more often than seen, the call being a loud "teacher, teach'—er, TEACH'—ER," getting louder toward the end. Nests on ground in woods, but visits bird baths in garden.

WAXWINGS

Waxwing, Bohemian—Larger than a sparrow, brownish-buff on back, prominent crest. Yellow band at tip of tail. Winters occasionally in North Central states and north-east; south to northern California.

Waxwing, Cedar—Larger than a sparrow, smaller than Bohemian waxwing. Clean-cut, brownish-buff bird with a prominent crest. Yellow band across end of tail. Will feed in yard on cherries (sometimes called "cherry-bird"), and other tree fruits. May visit feeders in winter.

WHIP-POOR-WILL see Goatsuckers

WOODPECKERS

Woodpecker, Downy—About sparrow size. Black back with white bars and white patch running down middle of back. White beneath. Male with red spot on back of head. Common garden woodpecker, nesting in tree cavities or birdhouses. Feeds readily on suet and fat.

Woodpecker, Hairy—Smaller than robin, larger than downy. Black on top with white bars. White back, white underneath. Male, red spot on back of head. Heavy bill. Nests in tree cavities, or occasionally in birdhouses. Will visit feeders in winter.

Woodpecker, Lewis's—Almost robin size. Black back and head. Reddish belly, gray band around neck. Western woodpecker, nesting in tree cavities.

Woodpecker, Red-headed—Smaller than robin. Entire head, red. Black back, white beneath. White patches on back edge of wing. Nests in tree cavities, and occasionally in birdhouses. May visit feeders in north.

Flicker—Larger than a robin. Brownish back and white rump as it flies distinguish the flicker. Underwings are yellow. Black band across breast and red patch on back of neck. Frequently seen feeding on ants on lawn, or hammering on tree in typical woodpecker manner (which it is). Sometimes nests in birdhouses.

WRENS

Wren, Carolina—Sparrow size. Reddish brown above, yellowish-brown below, white stripe over eye. Nests from southern New England south, in trees or in crevices in buildings. May visit tangles and thickets around garden or yard.

Wren, House—Smaller than a sparrow. Grayish, brownish in color, cocks tail over back as it gurgles its musical song. Common wren of orchards and yards where it nests in birdhouses, holes in buildings or almost anywhere it can find a hole. Has even nested in pants pockets on clotheslines. Audubon has painted a wren nesting in an old hat left hanging outdoors.

YELLOWTHROAT see **Warblers**

DUCKS

Mallard—Medium sized duck (large for a wild duck). Male, green head, gray back, white ring around neck, reddish breast and white tail. Female, brownish all over, blue wing patch, white tail. Common duck in park ponds. Will feed readily on corn, and becomes quite tame.

Black Duck—About mallard size. Dark brown all over, with lighter head, and white underwings that flash when bird flies. Common in winter in park ponds and other open water. Feeds on corn rather readily, and will become quite tame.

Baldpate (Wigeon)—About mallard size. Male, brownish on back, gray colored head, and a distinctive white crown (bald pate). Greenish tinge to sides of head. Blue bill. White patch on fore edge of wings. Female, brownish, gray head, blue bill. Winters from Long Island south and along Pacific Coast. May be seen on ponds where it feeds with mallards and blacks.

Pintail—About mallard size, but slimmer. Male, white breast, brown head, grayish on back. White line running into side of head. Pointed tail, cocked upwards. Female, brownish, shorter pointed tail, slender neck. Winters along Pacific Coast, and from Long Island south, where it may be seen on ponds and lakes.

Shoveller—Smaller than mallard. Male, black on top of back and rear. White breast and sides of back. Greenish head, long broad bill. Rusty sides. Female, dull brown, but distinctive shoveller bill. Winters on ponds, like mallards. Will eat corn left in shallow water.

Wood Duck—Smaller than mallard, and the male is most beautifully colored duck. In winter, iridescent on back, rusty red breast, buffy sides. Head a striking pattern of dark and white with crest. Female, dark brownish, white belly, crest on head, and white patch around eye. Nests in forests and along streams and occasionally in birdhouses. On farms will nest reasonably near houses in tree cavities. Winters on ponds north to Illinois and Long Island, also Pacific states.

Teal, Green-winged—Small duck. Male, gray, brown head and white patch on front of wing. When flying, green wings, white belly are apparent. Female, small brown duck with green on wings. Probably smallest ducks to winter on ponds and lakes in parks and estates. May become tame, and feed on corn in shallow water.

CHAPTER 3

WANTED—MORE BIRD HOMES

As you become better acquainted with the birds around your home, you will soon find that their activities change with the seasons. Probably the most interesting time of year is spring and early summer when birds are nesting. For it is during this time that plumage is at its height of brilliance and songs at their best.

This is the time when the migrants coming north, stop in the yard to feed and rest. This is the time when the brilliant orange of the oriole flashes through the apple blossoms; when the scarlet of the tanager contrasts with the blossoms in the cherry tree; and the subtle coloring of the warblers lends added color to the garden. This is the time of year to get to bed early and up at the crack of dawn for somehow or other the beauty of these birds seems greatly enhanced in early light when dew still sparkles on the grass and the blooms and blossoms have not yet become faded by the hot sun.

Early morning, too, is the best time for bird songs, before the more mundane sounds of the neighborhood drown them out. The chorus of songs from the tree tops, of orioles, robins, tanagers, or warblers; thrashers, catbirds, thrushes and grosbeaks singing from the shrubs; and ovenbirds or towhees calling from the ground—all may have you running in circles for a while. But soon you can sort them out, and take them one at a time. Then you can enjoy bird songs in all their glory.

If it were not for one rather unfortunate human trait, neatness, many of the birds passing through in the spring might be staying to nest. But their needs are not found in the average yard, so they move on to other places.

Two things may be done to make the yard more attractive to birds. One is planting plants that provide shelter and cover, (See Chapter IV) and the other is setting out bird boxes and brackets. In nature these requirements are found in thickets, bushy places, and trees, alive or dead. Our neatness and the efficiency of tree surgeons have made it difficult for birds to find nesting sights around towns and villages. Thickets and dead trees do not fit into our schemes of landscaping. But substitutes may be found in artificial plantings and in bird boxes.

It seems incongruous, but it is true that our neatness means a greater cost in insecticides and sprays, for most of the hole-nesting birds that would nest in the dead trees around the garden or public parks are insect eaters, and statistics prove that they destroy a tremendous number of harmful insects. Not only must the adult birds eat, but when the young hatch they seem to have insatiable appetites that require an ever increasing supply of grubs.

We had read the statistics of scientists telling of the millions of insects destroyed by one pair of birds in a lifetime, but it was not until we watched one red-wing nest for two hours that we could really understand the economic importance of birds. We had hidden ourselves in a blind, and focused our glasses. There were three young in the nest.

The female bird came to the nest nineteen times the first hour, and fifteen times the second hour we watched. She had at least two insects—grubs or adult moths—each time. Sometimes she had three or four. As fast as she could, she poked the grubs down the open throats of her hungry young, and took off for another supply. We estimated that she did this for at least six hours a day, for the week or ten days the young were in the nest. That does not count the insects she ate herself, or those devoured by the male who, while we watched, alternated between a perch near the nest and a cherry tree a hundred feet away.

The much maligned English sparrow has also proved itself helpful as an insect destroyer—but this bird does not need help in finding nesting space. Several pairs nest in a crevice in the stucco on our home, and long and loud did we curse them as we washed the window under the nests. But on the windowsill we have a feeder, and on this feeder one day we found something that made us change our minds somewhat about the sparrow. The feeding tray was covered with the shells of Japanese beetles.

The next day we watched the birds to see how they caught those destructive imports from across the Pacific. The way they caught the beetles was interesting to see.

At that time, the beetles were making quick work of the leaves in our grape arbor. Thousands of them were turning the leaves into little more than veins and stems. But along came the sparrows, and although they did not do the job of the famous Utah gulls of a century ago, they certainly did help do away with thousands of the beetles.

The sparrows would perch in the lilac bush, then suddenly dart into the grapes. Up would fly a dozen or so beetles, and quick as a flycatcher, up would go the sparrow to catch one on the wing. Then back to the lilac bush until the beetles settled down, then back to the grapes for another meal.

Since then we have not encouraged more sparrows to nest, but neither have we discouraged them.

Our family of downy woodpeckers have proved their worth too, if only on one occasion. In late summer we were in the vegetable garden trying to save a late crop of beans from that inevitable pest, the bean beetle, when we thought we heard the call of a downy come from the corn patch. It seemed unlikely that a downy would be eating corn, but it was worth a look. We grabbed our glasses from their regular place on a fencepost and looked over the ripened golden bantam. Sure enough, there was a downy—not only one but the two, male and female. They were climbing each stalk, from the ground to the top, and were efficiently probing for grubs. Never did we feel better repaid for our efforts to keep those birds in the yards, for our first batch of corn showed unmistakable signs of borers, and we knew that each successive picking would be worse. We cannot say that the downies ate all the borers, but they must have found some, for we saw them there on many subsequent days.

Those three personal observations make it easy for us to understand the figures sent out by experts: That without birds, the damage by insects would be increased by some four hundred million dollars a year; that chickadees in the state of Michigan destroy eight billion insects each year; that the stomach contents of one white breasted nuthatcher contained more than sixteen thousand eggs of the cankerworm moth.

So, in addition to the aesthetic value of the birds that may nest in the yard, there certainly is an economic consideration.

But rare is the yard or garden that provides a natural nesting place for the more desirable of the hole-nesting species. As soon as a tree dies it is cut down. When a large limb dies, down it goes before the saw of a tree surgeon. And the downy woodpecker or flicker, upon whom falls the job of excavating many of the nesting holes for other birds, look to the woods for home sites.

Generally, woodpeckers make a new nest each year. That means that they leave last year's hole for the hole-nester with a weaker bill such as the chickadee, tree swallow, bluebird or wren. Of course, many of these birds will nest in rotted-out places instead of woodpecker homes, but sometime watch an old woodpecker hole and see what happens the next year.

The most interesting case we ever saw was at the Roosevelt Bird Sanctuary, maintained by the National Audubon Society, in Oyster Bay, Long Island. About six feet up from the ground in a dead oak, a downy had drilled out a nest. During the following fall, the sanctuary fell heir to an injured barn owl, which was placed in a large wire cage in front of the oak. The hole in the oak faced the cage, with about six inches between the tree and the wire.

When spring came, a pair of chickadees selected the hole for a nest, despite the fact that to enter it they had to fly through the cage, right under the nose of the owl. When we saw the nest, apparently the young had hatched, for the adult birds were constantly coming and going, through the wire, past the owl, out the other side of the cage, and back again.

It is doubtful if these birds were that hard up for a place to nest, for in the sanctuary were many bird boxes, and the surrounding country is covered with trees. Perhaps the chickadees had not been told the facts of life—that the owl would just as soon eat them as a mouse.

For several summers we have watched an abandoned orchard in upstate New York. It is perhaps fifteen years since the orchard was pruned or sprayed. It took about ten years for birds to take it over, but now nearly every other tree has a bird nesting in it—either in an old woodpecker hole or flicker hole, or in a rotted place where a branch blew off. In this orchard of two dozen trees, we counted ten nests—bluebirds, chickadees, downies, flickers, and white-breasted nuthatches.

It does not take much to encourage birds to nest—where dead trees are not practical, birdhouses will do the trick. There are many examples of very successful bird box projects. Some years ago, Mr. T. E. Musselman of Quincy, Illinois, noted the drop off in the number of bluebirds that nested locally around farms. He set out 102 bluebird houses along 40 miles of country road—on fenceposts chiefly. He found that 88 of these boxes housed bluebird families, and averaging four young to a nest, this meant some 352 more bluebirds to catch bugs, sing their warbling song from the orchard, and flash their blue and rust color among the blossoms in spring.

Following Mr. Musselman's lead, a troop of Boy Scouts recently developed a project that resulted in the construction of 150 birdhouses, which were set up along the country roads in Erie County, New York, in the midst of the apple country. A check later showed that more than four hundred young birds had been produced. The troop still continues the project by cleaning out the boxes every fall so that they will be ready for the coming spring.

Another group of Boy Scouts built tree swallow houses and placed them around the lake at their camp on Cape Cod. Tree swallows had not nested there before, but in the first season a dozen of the houses were used by these birds.

In addition to providing birds with nesting sites, boxes also provide shelter during the winter, for when icy winds blow and sleet and snow cover tree and shrub, birds may have a hard time in our clean and cleared gardens and towns. Margaret McKenny in *Birds in The Garden,* quotes the observation of one birder who saw thirty-one winter wrens take shelter in a birdhouse used in summer by a violet-green swallow. Thus it seems that bird boxes do double duty, and help in winter as well as summer to keep birds in our yards and gardens.

Birdhouse building has its satisfactions, but it also has its aggravations. One friend of ours had his troubles with house wrens. He remembered these cheerful little birds as they nested around the farm on which he had been raised. Now, when he lived in the suburbs, he wanted his children to be able to enjoy wrens as he had done.

He had never seen a wren in his town, but he felt that a few well-placed birdhouses might attract them. During a few winter nights he worked hard and long in his basement shop, making the finest kind of wren houses. He painted some, and stained others. He set them out in his rather small back and side yard. With the coming of spring he watched for wrens with more interest than he read the daily stock quotations. April came and went. No wrens. May passed by, and still no wrens. Then came the day. He was walking to catch the 8:02 when he heard a wren. The gurgling song came from a neighboring yard. He forgot the train and a 9:15 appointment. There was a wren, and he had not seen one in years. Quietly, he stalked through his neighbor's yard. He stopped and listened. There was the wren again, singing out beside the garage. He sneaked up behind a shrub and peered around. Yes, the wren was in the dwarf apple tree. As he watched, now stooping down, brief case under his arm, one hand outstretched to hold back a branch of the shrub, a movement on the garage windowsill caught his eye. A wren flew from the hole in the bottom of an old flowerpot that was resting upside down on the sill. They had passed up his houses for this nesting place. And as he turned around to resume his walk to the station, there was the neighbor and his family watching him out of the dinette window.

But not dismayed by his first failure, he tried again. This time he bought two wren houses from the Audubon Society. Surely the wrens would not pass them up.

Came spring again, and this time the wrens came to his yard. They tried out the boxes, and even perched on top of one to sing. But did they nest in them? They raised their families in a hole in a clothespost, out in a corner where they could not be seen from the house. But at least he had wrens in his yard, if not bats in his belfry as his neighbors had good reason to believe.

Probably the most interesting wren nests we saw were in a camp with which we were associated a few years ago. The camp had a rifle range which was an important part of its program. Every day a couple of dozen boys shot thousands of rounds into the log backstop. In the backstop were several places where knots had fallen out, leaving small holes. In two of these holes were nesting wrens. The targets were moved so that none but wild shots could possibly hit the nests. And that was enough protection for the birds. They continued nesting, flying in and out of their homes, whether firing was going on or not. The mere sound of rifles and the ping of lead flying into the backstop had no effect whatever.

As exasperating as was the experience of our friend with wrens, were the tribulations of another friend with purple martins. For eight years he tried to attract martins to his farm. The money he spent building martin houses, and traveling around looking at nesting colonies, would have paid for a new barn or new wing on the house. But he could not get martins to nest in his houses, even if the plans were approved by the U. S. Department of Agriculture and the Audubon Society. English sparrows nested in the martin house. Once a martin sat on top of the house—but no nests.

Finally, he sold his upstate New York farm and bought one on eastern Long Island. We were not sure, of course, and he will not admit it, but we think the chief reason for the change was a martin colony not too far from the new place. Before furniture was moved in, or the electricity hooked up, up went the martin house. But still no martins. Tree swallows nested in houses placed around the farm. Ospreys nested on an old wagon wheel placed on a pole down in the south corner. But no martins.

The story has a happy ending though, and some psychiatrist lost a good customer, for a more frustrated human being you never saw. But persistence paid off, and after eight years, our friend attracted a colony of martins to his farm.

This all goes to prove that just because you build and set out birdhouses, birds will not necessarily nest in them. But that is another of the thrills of back yard birding comparable to winning a blue ribbon with your prize petunias or catching your biggest trout.

Before you make any birdhouses, or even before you buy any, check over these rules of birdhouse construction. Some have a definite bearing on whether or not the birds you want will nest in them. Other rules will determine how many young fly out of the birdhouse—and that is the true test. No matter how pretty the house looks, or how well it will blend in your garden, if desirable birds do not use it and raise their young successfully, the house is not worth much.

First, make or buy houses for specific birds—wren houses, bluebird houses, chickadee houses or tree swallow houses. Do not just make or buy a birdhouse. Birds have certain size requirements, even as you and I.

Second, do not try apartment houses, except for martins. Most birds demand privacy and will drive away others of the same species that come too close to their homes.

Third, do not make the holes too large. Every bird has its own requirements. Make the hole to fit the bird, and no larger. English sparrows and starlings will use the house if the hole is large enough, and drive away the more desirable species.

Fourth, do not use tincans for birdhouses. The sun beating down on tin will heat up the inside and bake the young birds.

Fifth, do not set up too many houses in a small area. Generally, three or four to an acre is the largest number that will be used.

Sixth, do not hide the houses in dense foliage. They should be placed in open shade, on poles, tree trunks, or suspended from branches.

Seventh, clean out the houses after each season. Birds demand clean houses each year. This means that houses should have provisions for easy cleaning. Either the top or bottom should be hinged, so that they can be cleaned without the trouble of taking them down.

Eighth, all houses should be made so that they are well ventilated and easily drained of any rain water that may blow in. Slits just under the roof will supply ventilation, and a few holes drilled in the bottom will provide drainage. Birds like to be cool and dry and must be if the young are to be raised successfully.

Following are specifications for houses for some of the more common species, recommended by the U. S. Department of Agriculture:

1. Bluebird, Mountain Bluebird, Western Bluebird or House Finch.

Floor size	5 x 5 inches
Height of house	8 inches
Hole above floor	6 inches
Diameter of hole	1 ½ inches
Height above ground	5—10 feet

For bluebirds place houses in sunny places, in orchard or along roadsides. For house finch, place in yard or garden.

2. House wren, Carolina wren.

Floor size	4 x 4 inches
Height of house	6 or 8 inches
Hole above floor	6 inches
Diameter of hole	1 inch
Height above ground	5—10 feet

For Carolina wren, make hole 1⅛ inches. Set out houses in very early spring, not too close together.

3. Chickadees, Nuthatches, Titmice, Downy Woodpecker.

Floor size	4 x 4 inches
Height of house	8—10 inches
Diameter of hole	1⅛ inches
Hole above floor	6—8 inches
Height above ground	5—15 feet

For nuthatches, titmice and woodpecker, make hole 1¼ inches. All these birds prefer a bark-covered house. Use slab wood with bark on it, or drill hole through a log. For downies place some wood chips in bottom.

4. Tree Swallow, Violet-Green Swallow.

Floor size	5 x 5 inches
Height of house	6 inches
Diameter of hole	1½ inches
Hole above floor	5 inches
Height above ground	5—15 feet

Place these houses in the open on a post or dead tree.

5. Crested Flycatcher.

Floor size	6 x 6 inches
Height of house	8—10 inches
Diameter of hole	2 inches
Hole above floor	6—8 inches
Height above ground	8—20 feet

Nail bark over house and place in woods or orchard.

6. Flicker.

Floor size	7 x 7 inches
Height of house	16—18 inches
Diameter of hole	3 inches
Hole above floor	14 inches
Height above ground	8—20 feet

Make house of wood at least an inch thick. Sprinkle chips or shavings inside.

7. Screech Owl.

Floor size	8 x 10 inches
Height of house	12—15 inches
Diameter of hole	3¼ inches
Hole above floor	10 inches
Height above ground	10—30 feet

Rustic house is best, but even then it takes luck to get one to use the house.

Whether you buy bird boxes ready-made or make them yourself is a matter of preference. There are several reputable manufacturers of good houses who are as interested in birds as they are in their business. But there are many who just sell birdhouses. It is best to check houses over carefully before you buy them. But if you see any carrying the names Bishop, Hyde or Packard, you may be sure of getting a good house. There are undoubtedly others, but in our experience these manufacturers put out excellent products.

The National Audubon Society, 1000 Fifth Avenue, New York, N.Y., through its service department, sells approved houses of several concerns. Write to them for a catalog.

If your preference is making your own, as is ours, start with the one shown on page 72. It is designed for bluebirds and is the one used so successfully by Mr. Musselman in Illinois, and the Boy Scouts of Erie County, New York. The specifications may be changed slightly to make it suitable for other species of birds.

Use one-inch thick wood, which as you get it from the lumberyard is three-quarters to seven-eighths of an inch thick. If possible, use cypress because it will weather better and last longer. Use brass screws and hinges so they will not rust.

To make one house, you will need a piece of wood six inches wide (about five and three-quarters as it comes from the mill) and fifty-two inches long. Saw off a piece fourteen inches long for the backboard. Saw off a second piece five inches long for the top, and trim it down to five by five and a quarter inches. Then ripsaw the board for nineteen inches so you have a piece four inches wide. Cut this piece into two nine and one-half inch pieces for the sides. Saw a half inch triangle off of each side, so the top will slant toward the front.

Next, rip the board so you have a piece three and a quarter inches wide. Cut off a piece nine inches long for the front,

Top—Bluebird house similar to the Musselman design. It is easy to make and will attract other birds if made to slightly different specifications (see page 69).

Bottom—Tree Swallow house of a simple design and easily made in the home workshop.

and a piece three and one quarter inches square for the bottom. The bottom and the front fit inside of the sides. Center the sides on the backboard, and use screws to fasten in place. Use a hinge to attach the top as shown. Be careful drilling the hole so as not to split the front.

The other houses shown on pages 74, 77 are just as easily made. But use good wood and brass fittings, for best results.

If your artistic sense demands that your homemade houses be painted, use a good oil stain, preferably oak. A dull color that blends into the background seems best. Probably the best idea of all is to set out the house in the fall so it will weather by spring. But general rules all are easily broken and wrens may nest in a house the day you put it up.

Such houses as martin houses that stand in direct sun are best painted white to reflect heat instead of absorbing it. Others are best in a dark tone.

There are many birds that are attracted by bird boxes and will nest in them. There are others that nest around human habitations, that will not use birdhouses, but which you may help, nevertheless.

Robins will rarely nest on brackets—an open birdhouse, with floor, back and roof, but open sides. This same bracket doubles in the winter as a feeder. We have had one in a pear tree for ten years. For eight years, robins have nested under it and over it, but never in it. However, several birds use it as a feeder, so the time spent making it was not a total loss. But robins do use the nesting materials we set out for them. We have made a crude rack of coarse mesh chicken wire, which hangs on a low branch of the maple. In the rack we place short lengths of string, yarn, raveled rope and bits of thread.

Top—Shelf under eaves may provide nesting site for phoebes or swallows.

Lower left—Double-purpose bracket. In winter it serves as a suet rack or seed holder. In summer, robins may use it for nesting.

Center right—Woodpecker or chickadee house, easily made from slab wood or a hollowed log. Some birds prefer a natural-appearing house.

Both orioles and robins pick it clean during the nesting season.

On a recent trip to Florida we returned with a bag of Spanish moss. We hung it from the branches of our fruit trees, and found it later in a catbird nest, two robin nests, and a song sparrow nest. We do not know how much went to the English sparrows, up in the corner of the house.

We have heard of oriole nests that were made almost entirely of colored yarns left out as nesting material. We have seen a few pieces in nests, but the thought of a multicolored nest of reds, blues, yellows and greens is an enchanting one to say the least. Oh, for a Kodachrome of a male oriole in such a nest! But oriole nests being where they are—on the ends of the highest branches in elms—the possibilities of such a picture are rare indeed.

Phoebes too, are birds which will not nest in birdhouses, but which may be attracted to the yard. They have a liking for bridges, and many a country bridge over a stream or creek has its phoebe nesting on the stringers beneath. Many a house or outbuilding has a phoebe nesting up under the eaves, wherever there is a board or bracket to support the nest.

Some phoebes seem to return to the same place year after year with about the same regularity as the famous Capistrano swallows, so it is well worth while trying to capture their interest. A board nailed to the wall of the garage or house up under the eaves will support the nest, and if phoebes come once, before many years have gone by, a row of old nests will line the bracket.

Phoebes, like many other birds, raise more than one family per season, so the possibility is good for this bird being around for years to come. As far back as we can remember, phoebes have nested on the side of our cabin in the country, and now, at least twenty-five years later, we show our children the nest just as regularly as we looked for it at the same age. As we sit at breakfast or lunch, on May to August week ends, we watch the phoebes carrying.insects to their young. There are now six old nests lined up on that old board which some careless carpenter forgot to remove a quarter-century ago, and it seems like only last spring that we cleaned it off, for a new family to come.

Our barn up there in the mountains has long since caved in under a hundred years of wind and rain, and our short stays there have not made it worthwhile to rebuild it. But one of our fondest memories of that barn were the swallows that nested inside. The mud nests, plastered against the rafters up in the very peak, were wonderful to us. And how the bird could dart through a four by four diamond-shaped hole up near the ridge, always folding its wings the split second it came to the opening, was more than we could understand.

We wish now, we had the time spent then, watching and waiting for a swallow to miss the hole and crash into the barn. But such an accident never occurred.

Our present suburban garage is too hemmed in to attract these graceful birds, but a neighbor has a garage that is more in the open. He has cut holes in either end, high in the peak, and swallows have nested there for several years. It goes without saying that the peak itself is boarded on the inside to protect the cars beneath. Our neighbor has provided a place for swallows by building a "room" just under the ridge, about two feet deep.

A rather common, but seldom seen bird in some towns

Purple martin house. Martins are the only birds to nest in "apartment houses." This plan is similiar to a design made by the U.S. Department of Agriculture and has proved to be successful in many places.

these days is the barn owl. Originally nesting in hollow trees, this winged mousetrap has become adapted to civilization and nests in old barns and cupolas on private as well as public buildings. In some places they nest in church belfries, in another place in the chute of a coalyard. In a neighboring town to ours, they nested in the belfry of the local firehouse until the firemen felt that sirens and owls did not mix. Right in our town, we found a nest in an abandoned house. The home had been empty for several years, and most of the windows had long been shot out by juvenile marksmen with slingshot or air rifle.

A third-story room made a fine home for a pair of barn owls and only the housing shortage brought about the renovation of the old house and the dispossession of the owls. But for three years to our knowledge, the owls annually raised two or three young, and at a minimum of five mice daily, to feed parents and young, they easily paid their rent.

It is not recommended that one knock out the window of a house, or build a belfry to provide a home for wandering owls. But the top of a garage might be used or even the upper part of a barn, if an opening is made as an entrance.

Inviting barn owls is not an invitation to nightly choruses of hoots and weird calls. Barn owls are quiet owls, and you scarcely know they exist. They are active chiefly at night, from dusk till dawn, roaming over field and marsh, sometimes at long distances from their nests, searching for the mice and rats that make up their diet. They are not as easy as chickadees or bluebirds to attract, but they are far more interesting in our opinion.

Anyone with a moderate size yard or garden at their disposal—or a neighboring park where authorities will permit bird boxes—can have many interesting hours watching wild birds at home. But setting out bird boxes is only one way to make a garden attractive. The other way is to set out plants that provide food, cover and nesting sites.

CHAPTER 4

BACK YARD BIRD SANCTUARIES

THE best way to attract birds to the yard or garden is to plant a good selection of trees, shrubs and ground plants that provide food, cover and places to nest. Feeding stations, of course, will bring birds during winter. Bird baths may be used the year round. Bird boxes are used in spring and early summer. But for the largest number of birds for the greater part of the year, nothing is as desirable as the proper plantings of shrubs, vines or trees that meet the three main requirements of wild birds.

One of the most unfortunate aspects of the spread of civilization from city to suburb, and of the expansion of suburban communities, from the viewpoint of the back yard naturalist, is the destruction of bird habitats.

We once lived on the edge of a four-acre oak woods. Blueberries, cat brier, and young sassafras covered the ground. Orioles, tanagers, woodpeckers, thrushes and chickadees nested there every year. Warblers and vireos stopped there during migration. Except for a rare game of cowboys and

Indians, that woods was the birds'. But now a barren playground occupies the space and Bronx cheers or referees' whistles take the place of an oriole's warbling song and the tapping of the downies and flickers.

Another small oak woods nearby, where we once photographed ovenbirds, towhees, catbirds, night herons and wood thrushes, is now a mass of small houses. English sparrows are hard put to find food, especially since the old-fashioned milk wagon has been replaced by the products of General Motors or Chrysler.

It is not that we begrudge our youngsters a place to play, or our neighbors the opportunity of getting out of city apartments into the relative open country of the suburbs. We are happy for them. But what we do not understand is why a fringe of trees has no place around a ballfield; and why every inch of rich top soil must be scraped off before a house can be built.

I suppose it is more economical and efficient to cut down hundred-year-old oaks and maples; to bulldoze out the stumps, and to scrape off all the centuries' accumulation of leaf mold; then to build a few houses, put back a few inches of top soil, and plant a dozen or so ten-year-old saplings in straight lines down a street. Otherwise, why would it be so universal a practice in housing developments? If many of the original trees had been left there, and if the original top soil with its rich leaf mold had been left, how much easier it would be for the new homeowner to landscape his plot, and to grow plants other than pansies, zinnias and privet hedges.

The extremes to which modern builders go was illustrated in a large development on Long Island. Hundreds of homes were being built in the same manner as cars rolling off an assembly line. Every man had one small job to do. But the birdhouse erection crew, some five men, had a system to make efficiency experts swell with pride. When the houses had been completed, the birdhouse crew went to work.

There were no trees large enough to support even a wren house, so the bird boxes were placed on poles. Down one side of the street, through the back yards, went the holedigger with a regulation post holedigger. Five paces from the edge of each driveway, he quickly dug a hole two feet deep, neatly piling the dirt beside the hole. Meantime, down the street came a truck with ten-foot poles, all painted. On the end of each pole was a birdhouse, a miniature of the home itself. Needless to say, each birdhouse was suitably painted and ready for occupancy.

The poles were dropped off, one to a house. Then came the pole setter, who picked up the pole and set it in the hole, kicking in only enough dirt to hold the pole upright. Finally came the tampers who shoveled in the rest of the dirt, tamping it down firmly. A recent check showed only house sparrows using about two percent of the nesting boxes.

The interesting thing is, that all this effort went into a misguided attempt to get birds to nest where they had been nesting in great numbers for years. The unfortunate part of it is that no birds except house sparrows would ever nest in the boxes—they were just birdhouses, not built for any particular bird. If the same effort and money had been spent saving a few of the old trees, or even planting a few dogwoods or cedars, the results in the long run might have been much more desirable.

Over the years we have tried to make our yard and garden edges a substitute for the natural areas that once attracted so many birds. At the same time, any planting had to be consistent with family requirements of a back yard. Our results have been such that we can recommend the method to others who desire back yard sanctuaries. For in one nesting season we have had six nests in the yard—two robin nests, a song sparrow, a blue jay, a catbird, and a black-billed cuckoo. Several house sparrows nest on the house, but we do not count them, and a pair of starlings nested in a dead apple tree, but we did not count them for they have been there for years. In addition, on one spring week end, we counted forty-one different species feeding or resting in the yard, or dunking in the bird bath.

Our own experience, plus observations of other yards and reading of the experiences of others, has led to several conclusions that we feel safe in passing on.

First of all, the size of the yard does not make too much difference. Of course, the larger the area, the larger is the selection of plants you can use, and more different types of plant masses are possible. This is bound to result in more birds. But a surprising number of birds may be attracted to a small area. Not long ago, we saw a 40 x 40 yard in a heavily builtup section. That yard was surrounded by garages, houses and apartments, and how the birds could weave through the radio and television antennas, telephone wires and clotheslines is more than we know. But they do, and that small oasis attracts an unbelievable number of birds—almost a hundred a year. The yard is a veritable jungle. There is a narrow path down the middle, but from boardfence to boardfence, and from garage wall to backporch there is a mass of vines and shrubs that you cannot see through in summer. In that case it is the plants that attract the birds and not the size or unusual location of the yard. The important thing is the mass of plants that provide cover and food for migrating birds.

In general there are four aspects to planting.

First, certain trees and shrubs attract insects that in turn attract birds. Insects may be attracted by the blossoms or the leaves.

We have found that fruit trees such as apple, pear and cherry serve a triple purpose. They provide us with fruit, the blossoms are the color highlight of our garden, and the birds swarm to them during spring migration.

During the blossom season, one short week in May, the small orchard is alive with birds. Apparently, the insects attracted by the blossoms are particularly attractive to birds, for the apple blossom season does not always coincide with the peak of the migration waves of warblers, vireos, tanagers, orioles, and rose-breasted grosbeaks. But we can always count on seeing hundreds of birds in the trees when they are in bloom.

Several times, when birds have been scarce in the yard, we have gone to neighboring woods to find a great many. We have watched them fly over or through the yard stopping only for a few seconds. But when the blossoms are at their height, so are the birds.

It was during one blossom time that we set our back yard bird record—forty-one species in a single week end. Most of the birds were warblers, vireos and flycatchers, but thrushes, thrashers, tanagers and orioles also swelled the list. It was nothing to see a dozen male orioles in one small group of trees, or three or four tanagers in one tree. And if anyone knows a more spectacular color combination in nature, we would like to see it.

During the winter these same fruit trees are visited daily by downy woodpeckers, nuthatches and occasionally by a brown creeper or two. Two Norway maples, a row of young black walnuts, and two locusts also have attracted their share of these probing birds. For many insects spend the winter in the ridged bark of the trees where the woodpeckers and nut-hatchers can easily perch and dig them out.

Thus a careful selection of trees can fulfill more than one purpose. They can provide food for you, as well as birds; they can supply the desired shade and landscape effect that you desire. The list of plants at the end of this chapter was selected with these multiple uses in mind.

The effect on birds of insect control by spraying has long been debated by insecticide manufacturers and wildlife tech-nicians. Recent development of such sprays as DDT has given naturalists cause for concern since there is not much doubt but that these sprays in the hands of inexperienced persons may have a serious effect on some birds. We cannot answer the question from personal experience.

But we have not used DDT on our trees, rather we have relied on the older sprays to control the insects that would otherwise ruin our fruit crop. Fruit trees are not sprayed dur-ing blossom time anyway. Blossoms are pollinated by insects, and if insects are killed, no pollination, no fruit. It is the old story of the bees and the flowers. We do spray our trees ac-cording to a regular schedule, and we still have birds. We are not drawing conclusions, merely making an observation.

The second aspect of planting to attract birds is the food

supplied by the plants. Again it is easily possible to select plants that are desirable for home landscaping because of their blossoms and foliage, and at the same time attractive to birds as food plants. Happily some of the best trees for garden planting are also the best ones for birds, namely, flowering dogwood, flowering crab, shadbush and red cedar. Such plants as blueberries, raspberries and blackberries are also ideal for home gardens. The trees provide masses of blossoms that add color to the yard. The fruits of the berry bushes are well known. But the fruits of both trees and shrubs are excellent for birds. All of those plants are especially recommended by the Department of Agriculture for planting throughout the United States.

The effectiveness of natural food plants was brought home to us one fall day when we counted twenty-seven species in the yard in one afternoon. Finches made up the largest part, but hermit and wood thrushes, late warblers, towhees, catbirds, thrashers and waxwings were present in small numbers.

One corner of our garden is a tangle of cat brier, honeysuckle, Virginia creeper, sumac, sassafras and wild red cherry. We cannot take credit for planting it. It was there, and like Topsy, "just growed." All we did was keep it in bounds, and out of the tomato patch. Along the edges grow such "weeds" as ragweed and pokeweed or pokeberry. On that afternoon, the ragweed and pokeweed received the full attention of about a hundred sparrows, among them song sparrows, field sparrows, chipping sparrows, fox sparrows, white-throated sparrows, a Savannah sparrow, a vesper sparrow, and flocks of juncos and goldfinches. The pokeberry fruit went first, followed by the seeds of the ragweed. But the fruit of the Virginia creeper and honeysuckle were not overlooked by the waxwings and thrushes.

We had heard that the seeds of some of our common garden annuals would be eaten by birds. So with the first frost we changed our usual gardening routine. Instead of pulling out the blackened stalks, we left them in the garden, however ugly they looked. When an early snow covered the yard under some twenty inches, we had our answer.

When the snow had stopped, we broke open the heads of zinnias and marigolds and spread the seeds on the snow. We threw several partly broken heads into the feeders. The first flock of juncos, cowbirds, redwings, grackles and sparrows went for those seeds first. The commercial feed was second choice. Next year, we are planning a patch of flowers just to get seeds to feed birds.

Two other plants in our yard have fruit that has proved to be very attractive to birds. Both are easy to grow and are rather nice for home plantings. The first is bittersweet, and we like it particularly because the orange-red fruit is a nice fall and winter decoration for the house. The surplus on the vines along the fence is eaten by wintering robins and hermit thrushes. It is one of the best vines for planting around the home since it grows quickly and in almost any soil. Bittersweet will form a dense tangle, over a fence or shrub, and provides excellent cover and protection for birds.

Red mulberry is another tree that we have found easy to grow and very attractive to robins, jays, thrashers, catbirds and thrushes. The black fruit is messy as it drops off the tree, but fruiting about the same time as our cultivated cherry, it attracts birds away from the cherry. But one hint is in order if you plant a mulberry and if birds eat the fruit. Do not hang laundry on a line too near the tree. The birds flying over the clothesline to and from the tree are quite likely to drop the purplish-black berries, from one end or the other, right in the middle of a freshly laundered pillowcase or white shirt. The stain is difficult to remove. We know from experience.

The third reason for planting is to provide cover or shelter for birds. There are several plants that are ideal for this purpose, and at the same time excellent for certain landscaping effects.

One of the best examples of such a planting that we have seen is a hemlock hedge about eight feet high, eight feet through and forty feet long. It serves to screen a living-room from the street, but it provides the best kind of cover for birds. In ten minutes one winter afternoon we saw fox sparrows, white-throated sparrows, chickadees, a hermit thrush, two cardinals, a brown thrasher, a catbird and a song sparrow in that one hedge. There were several feeders in the yard where these birds fed, and the hedge provided a fine shelter when danger threatened, or when the cold winds blew. From the picture window of the house, that hedge makes an ideal background for a border flowergarden, and several specimen azalea shrubs.

In our own yard a privet hedge, planted as a combination windbreak, snow fence and screen, also provides cover for the birds that feed in our feeders. At first, we had placed our feeders in the open. The birds seemed reluctant to use them, but when we moved them nearer the hedge, they immediately became popular. We still have feeders in the open, for a better view from the house. But they are never used if the others are kept stocked. We saw the reason one day when a sharp-shinned hawk appeared on the top of the clothes-pole.

As the hawk came to his perch, the birds scattered and flew into the hedge. The English sparrows flew up and then down to shelter. The juncos, tree sparrows and song sparrows flew along the ground until they reached cover. The hawk perched and watched, and the song birds apparently forgot him as they flew back to the feeder. Suddenly, down swooped the hawk. Up flew the English sparrows, and the hawk took one on the wing. The other birds had flown into the hedge.

Since cats are greater enemies of birds than hawks, the birds in the yard need adequate cover from those animals. Evergreens are excellent because the branches are close together, thus making it difficult for cats to climb after the birds. Almost any dense shrub will provide shelter from enemies, but the shrubs and small trees that probably are best are the evergreens—spruces, cedars, yews and some pines, since they will also provide shelter from cold winds, sleet and snow.

The fourth reason for planting is to provide nesting sites for birds.

When it comes to nesting, two things, in general, determine where birds will nest, and whether or not they will nest. (This applies to birds that will nest usually in the yard or garden). One is the type of cover available—dense cover as is found in evergreens or dense thickets; and the height above the ground of suitable branches, forks, or crotches, with suitable cover, on which nests may be built. This combination of altitude and cover is very important.

Song sparrows, for example, which commonly nest in back yard sanctuaries, will nest on the ground, or up to a height of three or four feet. But they demand a rather thick growth. In many places, rambler roses have proved to be ideal for nesting sites.

In our yard, we have one clump of ramblers that has grown into a very dense mass. All we do is cut off the long runners that reach out to new heights every year. The bush itself is now about seven feet through, and six feet high. Proper care would undoubtedly result in more roses, but as it is, we get a reasonable number of blooms every year. More important to us, though, is the inevitable song sparrow nest that is right in the middle. These birds raise two families each season, so from early May until late July, we can enjoy the song of the male, and watch the active family life of these interesting birds—right from a dining-room window.

Robins, another common back yard nester, are not quite so demanding. They nest from five or six feet to twenty feet up, and in any of three trees in our yard. For three years one pair selected the blue spruce, and obligingly enough, built the nest within easy view of our upstairs window. Another pair usually nests in an apple tree, about ten feet up in a sturdy crotch, some hundred feet from the spruce. In other years, we have seen a nest in the Norway maple.

Catbirds prefer a dense thicket, and may nest from three or four feet off the ground to twenty feet up. Our nesting catbirds usually select a wild cherry in the cat brier-honey-suckle tangle, and build their nest in the first large fork of the trunk. In other years though, they have nested close to the ground in a small sumac.

Thrashers, too, prefer a dense thicket, and if you want cardinals, a thicket is almost a must. Of course, there are exceptions to all these general rules. Robins have nested on windowsills, tailboards of trucks, under the hoods of old cars and in all sorts of unexpected places. But we cannot rely on such nesting places, and must try to duplicate in back yard plantings, situations that are attractive to birds in the *natural* habitats.

Blue jays will nest in evergreens, such as grow around homes and garden edges, and may nest from three or four feet up, to the very top of the tree. In our yard, jays have nested in a privet hedge in back of the garage and in the wild cherry along the fence row. In other yards, we have seen nests in white pine, at about eye level, in blue spruces twenty feet up, and even on a low branch of a sycamore. Generally, though, they need more adequate cover and dense shade than they get on the more spreading trees.

In general, garden plants and shrubs that are planted in masses to make thickets and provide rather heavy shade from the ground level to a height of ten or fifteen feet offer the best opportunities for attracting nesting birds. The larger such an area can become, the better. But even a small thicket is better than none.

The ground itself in such an area should be left alone. It is a great temptation to rake out the fallen leaves and clean up such places. But the accumulation of leaves on the ground, over a period of years, makes a rich soil, and the resulting ground cover with its insect population is very good for birds.

If it is decided that plantings can be made to provide cover, food and nesting places for birds, as well as a more pleasant looking yard or garden, here are some suggestions for selecting plants.

The list of plants that follows has been based on several sources: personal observation and experience; lists published by the Wildlife Research Bureau of the U. S. Department of Agriculture; a list published by the National Audubon Society, with the cooperation of the New York State School of Forestry; and lists developed by Margaret McKenny in her excellent book *Birds in The Garden*. Latin names were taken from Gray's *New Manual of Botany*, and are included because of the difference in common names in different parts of the country, and even among different people in the same section of the country. Shadbush (*Amelanchier canadensis*) for example, is also called service berry, June cherry, June berry and several other names, depending upon where you are, and with whom you are talking.

At any rate, before starting to plant, unless you know your plants, it is an excellent idea to talk with an expert— and such advice is free in most sections of the country. Drop a card to your County Agent (found in telephone directory under State name, Agriculture Department); U.S. Agricultural Extension Agent or State Conservation Department representative.

Find out which plants are suited for your locality and soil. Then make a selection, based on your ideas of how your yard or garden should be landscaped. But keep in mind the requirements of the birds, if that is one of your purposes. Then make a rough sketch of the area to be planted and sketch in the plants, all the way from ground cover to trees.

In most cases, where possible, it is better to buy nursery stock for such plantings than to try to find your own plants in the wild. First of all, transplanting can be a tricky business unless you are experienced, and secondly, few landowners appreciate your digging up their shrubs, however high your motives. Of course, with permission, and with experience, transplanting is an excellent way to build up your garden, and for some plants it is necessary.

A second general rule is to stick to native plants as far as possible. Some exotics fit in very well, but generally it is more desirable to have the garden resemble the surrounding natural areas as closely as possible.

In transplanting from the wild to the garden, or from one part of the garden to another, the best time is spring or fall. Try to plant the new shrub in the same degree of shade or sun in which it was growing originally. Water it well before moving, so the soil sticks to the roots, and avoid letting the roots dry out or become exposed to sunlight. Take plenty of soil along with the plant, and drop soil and all in a previously dug hole. Water it well for a few days, and in case of a dry spell, water it once or twice a week for several weeks.

The best results in attracting birds come from planting in masses—that is large areas, where there are varieties of plants, from ground plants to trees, growing in one mass. A tree here and a shrub there, with a few vines in between, will not be too effective.

Generally, mass plantings are possible along fences, or property boundaries, or as screens across the yard to blot out the view of the service area of the yard—clotheslines, garages and out-buildings, garbage cans and the like. Fence corners are particularly good places to let a wild tangle develop. Backgrounds for the flowergarden can frequently be mass plantings of evergreens or other shrubs attractive to birds. An occasional specimen of dogwood, shadbush, or mountain ash will be effective since these are largely used as food plants.

With a careful selection of plants to provide cover, food and nesting sites for birds, the last requirement of a back yard sanctuary is to exclude cats. We know that many cat-lovers and cat society members will climb all over us in righteous wrath when we say that the best way to exclude cats is to eliminate them. But we sincerely believe, from experience with our own cats and observations of other people's, that once a cat becomes a bird-killer, there is no cure. If cats killed for food it would be one thing, but the average family pet is well fed at home and kills birds just for recreation. We have watched many cats stalk and kill garden birds; then walk off and leave the remains, to kill again within an hour. Young birds just out of the nest are particularly easy prey for stalking tabbies, and robins, song sparrows, catbirds, orioles, and thrashers are especially easy for cats to get.

One way to protect birds is supposed to be by tying a bell around the cat's neck. This, theoretically, will warn the bird of the cat's approach. But did you ever watch a cat stalk a bird? Its movements are so slow that rarely will the bell ring. It may click once in a while, but that will scarcely frighten a feeding bird.

Probably the best way to protect birds is with a catproof

fence. This means a close-mesh wire fence with pipe fence-posts. Wooden posts are out, because cats can climb them. The fence must be eight or ten feet high, with an overhang at top. The overhang must be a foot wide and so constructed that a cat cannot climb over it. But for the average home-owner, such a fence is quite costly, especially since it must extend around the entire garden. For the smallest hole or opening is large enough to admit a cat.

A catproof fence around our garden would cost some eight hundred dollars, and since we plan on moving sometime, it did not seem wise to invest in such a fence. We tried one or two other methods.

After watching cats kill birds at the feeders and at the bird bath, and after hitting them with stones, an air rifle and other weapons, only to have them return within the hour, we built a boxtrap. It was baited with fish, and once the cat went inside and tripped the trigger he was there to stay.

We prepared some notices on baggage tags, reading to the effect that this cat was quite unwelcome in our yard because it killed birds. We asked the owner to keep the cat at home. Usually the scheme worked. If a few days later the cat came back without the tag tied to its collar, or around its neck, we felt sure the owner had read it. When we trapped the cat a second time (proving the stupidity of cats) we attached a second notice. Like the second notice from a bill collector, it was in slightly stronger language. If this notice failed, the third warning was the "or else." The fourth time we caught the cat, we took it to the proper authorities for forwarding to the "Cat Valhalla," where there is a bird in every bush.

If a cat came around for three or four days with the tag

still on it, it was apparently a stray, without a home. The second time we caught it, it was taken away. Cats that used our cold frame or garage as a maternity ward were promptly dispatched, upon capture, to the gas chamber or whatever means are taken for disposing of cats.

This process has gone on now for six years. We have not yet been hailed to court or even been cursed at by neighboring cat-lovers. We have come to the conclusion that people who like their cats will keep them home; those that do not are looking for an easy way out, and that is us.

(We understand, from legal counsel, that we are well within our rights, according to the conservation laws of our state, in disposing of bird-killing cats. The only evidence necessary is the dead bird. It might be well to check, however, before indiscriminate cat elimination. But our trapping and tagging method seems safe enough.)

The following list of plants has already been described. The numbers at the left of each plant name refer to the groups of states in which the plant is native and in which it is most easily grown. That does not necessarily mean that if your state is not listed, that the plant will not grow there. Neither does it mean that the plant will definitely grow in your yard if your state is listed. These geographical references can serve only as a general guide. Different climates even within a state, different soil formations, amount of rainfall, and altitude all are determining factors. Use the list for general reference and consult local experts before making final selections.

The plants marked with an asterisk (*) are those recommended by the U. S. Department of Agriculture as being most attractive to birds throughout the United States. The birds listed as eating the fruits of those plants are also taken from Deparment of Agriculture leaflets.

State Groupings

1

Maine	Pennsylvania	Illinois
New Hampshire	Delaware	Michigan
Vermont	Maryland	Wisconsin
Massachusetts	Virginia	Minnesota
Rhode Island	West Virginia	Iowa
Connecticut	Kentucky	Missouri
New York	Ohio	
New Jersey	Indiana	

2

Arkansas	Tennessee	North Carolina
Louisiana	Alabama	South Carolina
Mississippi	Georgia	Florida

3

Oklahoma	Texas

4

North Dakota	Nebraska
South Dakota	Kansas

5

Montana	Wyoming	Colorado

6

Arizona   New Mexico

7

Utah   Nevada

8

California

9

Washington   Idaho   Oregon

Vines and Ground Cover

1, 4, 5   BEARBERRY (*Arctostaphylos uva-ursi*)
7, 8, 9   Low growing, creeping, evergreen shrub. Whitish
pink flowers, red fruit. Grows in acid soil, in open
shade.

Eaten by about thirty kinds of birds, especially
ruffed grouse, fox sparrow, solitaire and Rocky
Mountain jay.

1   BITTERSWEET (*Celastrus scadens*)
Shrubbery vine, orange fruit. Grows in open or
shade, up trees, or along fences, in any soil.
Eaten by hermit thrush, robin, bluebird and bobwhite.

1, 4, 5, 9   BUNCHBERRY (*Cornus canadensis*)
Small shrub. Red fruit. Grows in acid soil in shade.
Fruit eaten by ruffed grouse, pheasant, bobwhite,
prairie chicken, pine grosbeak.

1, 2   CAT BRIER (*Smilax glauca; S. rotundifolia; S. hispida*) Thorny vine, bluish-black fruit. Grows in any soil or shade. Forms dense thickets. Provides good cover, nesting sites and food.

Eaten by about forty kinds of birds, including robin, hermit thrush, cardinal, thrasher and catbird.

1, 2, 9   DEWBERRY (*Rubus flagellaris; R. hispidis; R. trivialis*)

Slender vine (*R. flagellaris*) growing in open as ground cover; black fruit. Growing in wet places (*R. hispidis*) Eaten by several sparrows, grouse, thrashers, thrushes, robin, waxwing, catbird, towhee, mockingbird.

1, 9   CROWBERRY (*Empetrum nigrum*)
*   Low evergreen shrub, black fruit. Grows in open and in sandy soil.

Eaten by forty kinds of birds, including pine grosbeak and snow bunting.

1, 2, 4,   WILD GRAPE (*Vitis labrusca; V. cordifolia; V. vul-*
5, 6, 7,   *pina; V. Arizonica;* others)
8 *   Large vine similar to cultivated grapes. Grows in any soil, in shade or open.

Eaten by eighty-seven kinds of birds, including ruffed grouse, bobwhite, northern and red-shafted flickers, pileated and red-bellied woodpeckers, eastern kingbird, mockingbird, catbird, brown thrasher, robin, wood thrush, veery, eastern and western bluebirds, cedar waxwing and cardinal.

1, 2, 3,   HONEYSUCKLE (*Lonicera sempervirens; L. albiflora;*
4, 5, 6,   others)

7, 8, 9   Climbing vine, red fruit. Grows in open or open
    *   shade, any soil. Forms thickets and good cover for
            birds. Eaten by eighteen kinds of birds including
            bobwhite, catbird, brown thrasher, robin, hermit
            thrush, pine grosbeak, white-throated sparrow.

1   GROUND JUNIPER (*Juniperus communis*)
            Low growing, evergreen shrub. Bluish fruit. Grows
            in acid soil in open.
            Eaten by robin, finches, bluebird, flicker.

1, 2, 3   PARTRIDGEBERRY (*Mitchella repens*)
    *   Low growing evergreen vine, with red fruit. Grows
            in acid soil in open or full shade.
            Eaten by ten kinds of birds, but especially the ruffed
            grouse.

1, 2, 3,   POKEWEED (*Phytoloca americana*)
6 *   A plant growing from three to eight feet high, with
            purple fruit in long clusters. Grows in garden as a
            weed, in open or semi-shade in rich soil.
            Eaten by fifty-two kinds of birds, among them
            mourning dove, flicker, eastern kingbird, mocking-
            bird, catbird, robin, hermit, olive-backed and gray-
            cheeked thrushes, eastern bluebird and cardinal.

1, 2, 5,   WILD SARSAPARILLA (*Aralia nudicaulis*)
9 *   Woodland ground plant with blackish fruit. Grows
            in shade, in rich acid soil.
            Eaten by sixteen kinds of birds, including bobwhite
            and robin.

1, 4, 5,   WILD STRAWBERRY (*Fragaria virginiana; others*)
7, 8, 9   Low plant, similar to cultivated varieties. Grows in
    *   open or in open shade, in rich soil.

Eaten by fifty-two kinds of birds, including catbird, brown thrasher, robin, wood thrush and towhee.

1, 5, 7,   Wintergreen or Checkerberry (*Gaultheria pro-*
9   *cumbens; G.*
   humifosa)

Low growing evergreen shrub. Red fruit. Grows in open or dense shade in acid soil.

Eaten by several birds, including grouse, pheasant, and wren-tit.

1, 2, 3,   Virginia Creeper (*Parthenocissus quinquefolia;*
4, 5, 7,   others)
8, 9 *   Long growing vine with blackish fruit. Grows in good soil in open or shade. Provides good nesting sites and food.

Eaten by thirty-eight kinds of birds, including flicker, red-bellied and red-headed woodpeckers, yellow-bellied sapsucker, tufted titmouse, mockingbird, brown thrasher, robin, hermit, olive-backed and gray-cheeked thrushes, eastern bluebird, red-eyed vireo, scarlet tanager, evening grosbeak, purple finch.

1   Matrimony Vine (*Lycium halimfolium*)

Shrubby vine with long drooping branches. Introduced from Europe. Grows around houses in good soil. Provides good cover and nesting site for birds.

Shrubs

1, 5   Arrowwood (*Viburnum dentatum*)

Tree-like shrub growing to twelve feet. Requires

moist soil and sun. Attractive for garden or yard. Provides good cover, nesting sites and food.

Eaten by more than thirty kinds of birds, including rose-breasted grosbeak, bluebird, robin, catbird, grouse and thrasher.

1   BLACK ALDER (*Ilex verticillata*)

Shrub growing to eight or ten feet, with red fruit. Requires rich, wet soil in sun or shade. Attractive shrub for yard, if it will grow there.

Eaten by grouse, waxwing and bluebird.

1, 2, 3,   BLACK HAW (*Viburnum prunifolium;* others)

4, 5 *   Grows to fifteen feet. No special soil or other requirements. Has blackish fruit. Provides good cover, nesting sites and food for birds.

Eaten by thirty-five kinds of birds, including ruffed grouse, yellow-billed cuckoo, flicker, catbird, brown thrasher, robin, eastern bluebird, cedar waxwing, rose-breasted grosbeak, purple finch.

4, 5, 6,   BUFFALO BERRY (*Shepherdia argentea; S. canadensis*)

7, 9 *   Grows to fifteen feet (*S. Argentea*) with red fruit. Thorns make it a good hedge. Provides cover, nesting sites and food. Growing to four feet is *S. canadensis.*

Eaten by eighteen kinds of birds, including sharp-tailed grouse, pine grosbeak.

1, 8   BURNING BUSH (*Euonymus atropurpurens; E. europaeus*)

STRAWBERRY BUSH (*E. Americanus*)

Shrubby tree, growing to twenty feet. Reddish

fruit. Grows in light, dry soil in sun. Provides fair cover, but good nesting sites for birds.

Eaten by tanager, robin, thrushes and other birds.

1, 2, 3, DOGWOOD (*Cornus alternifolia; C. Amomum; C.*
4, 5, 6, *paniculata; C. stolonifera; C. florida; C.*
7, 8, 9 *rugosa; C. asperifolia; C. Baileyi; C. oc-*
* *cidentalis; C. Californica; C. Nuttali;* others)

Growing as shrubs to small trees, depending upon variety, with attractive flowers and fruits. Ideal for planting in yard, but use kinds that grow locally. Provides fair cover and nesting sites, but fruit is excellent as food for birds.

Eaten by more than ninety kinds of birds, including such desirable species as ruffed grouse, bobwhite, northern and red-shafter flickers, downy woodpecker, eastern bluebird, catbird, brown thrasher, robin, wood, hermit, olive-backed and gray-cheeked thrushes, cedar waxwing, red-eyed and warbling vireos, cardinal, evening and pine grosbeaks, purple finch, house finch, and white-throated and song sparrows.

1, 2, 3, ELDER (*Sambucus canadensis; S. melanocarpa; S.*
4, 5, 6, *coerulea;* others)
7, 8, 9 An attractive shrub for background or borders of
* yard. Grows to twelve feet. Purplish-black fruit. Grows in damp soil, in shade or sun. Provides good cover, nesting sites and food.

Eaten by one hundred or more birds, including valley quail, flicker, red-headed woodpecker, eastern and Arkansas kingbirds, black phoebe, wren-tit, mockingbird, catbird, brown and California thrashers, robin, olive-backed thrush, eastern and western bluebirds, phainopepla, red-eyed vireo, rose-breasted grosbeak, black-headed grosbeak, California towhee and white-crowned sparrow.

1, 2, 3   HERCULES-CLUB (*Aralia spinosa*)
Thorny shrub, growing to twenty feet or more. Prefers moist soil.
Eaten by grosbeaks, thrushes, grouse, jay and sparrows.

1, 2, 3   HOLLY (*Ilex opaca*)
*
Evergreen shrub or tree. Red fruit. Provides fair cover and nesting sites for birds. Very attractive for planting in yard.
Eaten by forty kinds of birds, among them ruffed grouse, bobwhite, valley quail, flicker, yellow-bellied sapsucker, mockingbird, catbird, brown thrasher, robin, hermit thrush, eastern bluebird, cedar waxwing.

1, 4, 5   NANNYBERRY (*Viburnum lentago*)
An attractive shrub for the yard or garden, requiring moist soil, open shade or sun. Grows to thirty feet. Has blue-black fruit. Provides good nest sites and food. Eaten by cedar waxwing, robin, flicker, rose-breasted grosbeak, grouse, hermit thrush and bobwhite.

1, 2, 3,   WILD ROSE (*Rosa Carolina; R. setigera; R. rugosa;*
4, 5, 6,   *R. macauni; R. woodsi; R. nutkana;*
7, 8, 9   others)

*   Make attractive hedges or fence rows for yard. Grow on trellises or as low shrubs. Provide cover and nesting sites, and excellent food for many birds. Eaten by forty kinds of birds including grouse, prairie chicken, bobwhite, solitaire, pheasant, thrushes, robin and cardinal.

1, 4, 5,   SNOWBERRY (*Symphoricarpos albus; S. racemosus*)
6, 9 *   Low growing shrub with small flowers, but attractive white fruit. Grows in shade. Provides fair cover and nesting sites and good food for birds.
Eaten by more than thirty birds including grosbeaks, varied thrush, and sharp-tailed grouse.

1, 2, 3   WITHE ROD (*Viburnum cassinoides*)
Attractive shrub, growing to ten feet, with white flowers and black fruit. Requires moisture and sun. Provides fair cover and nesting sites, and good food. Eaten by forty kinds of birds, including grouse, thrasher, thrushes, purple finch, cardinal and jay.

1, 2, 3,   BLUEBERRY (*Vaccinium corybosum; V. pennsyl-*
4, 5, 6,   *vanicum; V. myrsinites; V. hirsutum;*
7, 8, 9   *V. oreophilum; V. membranaceum;*
*   *V. occidentale; V. ovatum; V. parvi-*
               folium; others)
Shrubs growing from two to fifteen feet, depending upon variety and location. Generally require sandy, acid soil and sunlight. Generally easily grown in garden or yard. Fruit prized by man as well as birds. Eaten by about one hundred birds, including ruffed grouse, valley quail, eastern bluebird, black-capped chickadee, tufted titmouse, catbird, brown thrasher,

robin, hermit thrush, eastern kingbird, cedar waxwing, orchard oriole, pine grosbeak and towhee.

2, 3   FARKLEBERRY (*Vaccinium arboreum*)
Evergreen shrub, growing to twenty feet 'or more. Grows in acid soil and has black fruit.
Eaten by quail and mockingbirds as well as other birds.

7   WHORTLEBERRY (*Vaccinium scoparium*)
Low growing shrub in blueberry family. Small reddish fruit.
Eaten by waxwings, pine grosbeaks, thrushes and other birds.

1, 2   BLACK CHOKEBERRY (*Aronia arbutifolia*)
*   RED CHOKEBERRY (*A. melanocarpa*)
Black chokeberry grows to three or four feet. Red chokeberry grows to ten feet. Attractive plants for garden with showy white flowers and beautiful fruit. Prefers moist, rich soil.
Eaten by twenty kinds of birds including brown thrasher and meadowlark.

1, 3   CORALBERRY (*Symphoricarpos arbiculatus*)
An excellent small shrub for the garden. Grows to five feet, with small white flowers, and dark red fruit. Ideal for planting on banks. Requires shade and rocky soil.
Eaten by many birds including grouse, pheasants and grosbeaks.

1, 2   DANGLEBERRY (*Gaylussacia frondosa*)
An attractive shrub with bluish fruit. Requires moist, acid soil.

Eaten by blue jay, catbird, grouse, quail, grosbeaks, and waxwings.

1   HOBBLEBUSH (*Viburnum alnifolium*)

An attractive shrub growing to eight feet. Flowers early and has purplish-black fruit. Prefers moist soil and shade.

Eaten by grouse, thrushes, thrashers, red-eyed vireos, and grosbeaks.

1, 4, 8   BLACKBERRY (*Rubus canadensis; R. frondosus; R. allegheniensis; R. macropetalus*)

An easily grown shrub, but must be kept under control or it will overrun the yard. Fruit well known as source of jams and jellies. Forms thickets that provide fair cover and nesting sites.

Eaten by nearly one hundred and fifty kinds of birds including house finch, thrushes, quail, sparrows, grosbeaks, robin, bluebird. Blossoms attract hummingbirds.

1, 2, 3,   RASPBERRY (*Rubus odoratus; R. deliciosus; R. me-*
4, 5, 6,   *lanalasius*)
7, 8, 9
  *

An easily grown shrub for the garden or yard, depending upon the variety. Fruit prized by man, but a few may be left for birds, or vice versa. Indigo buntings may sometimes nest in raspberry thickets. Eaten by about one hundred and fifty species of birds, including ruffed grouse, bobwhite, flicker, red-headed woodpecker, eastern kingbird, tufted titmouse, wren-tit, mockingbird, catbird, brown thrasher, robin, wood and olive-backed thrushes, eastern bluebird, cedar waxwing, red-eyed vireo, orchard and Baltimore orioles, cardinal, rose-breasted, black-headed and pine grosbeaks, red-eyed, spurred and California towhees, white-throated, fox and song sparrows.

1, 2, 3
*
SPICEBUSH (*Benzoin aestivale*)
An attractive shrub for the garden or yard, especially so in fall. Prefers shade and some moisture. Eaten by seventeen kinds of birds among them being the eastern kingbird, wood thrush, veery and red-eyed vireo.

1
MAPLE-LEAFED VIBURNUM (*Viburnum acerfolium*)
Especially attractive in fall because of purplish fruit. This shrub is easy to grow, and needs a dry soil. Will grow in shade or sun.
Eaten by many birds, among them being the cedar waxwing, robin, grouse, thrushes and finches.

1, 2
WINTERBERRY (*Ilex laevigata*)
A shrub growing to six feet, with reddish fruit. Prefers moist soil and shade.
Eaten by many birds.

1, 2, 3
*
BAYBERRY (*Myrica caroliniensis*)
An attractive shrub for the garden or yard (if you live along sea or lake shore). Waxy berries are quite fragrant. Provides fair shelter and nest sites. Requires sandy soil.
Eaten by eighty-five kinds of birds including bobwhite, flicker, downy woodpecker, eastern phoebe, tree swallow, black-capped chickadee, Carolina wren, catbird, brown thrasher, hermit thrush, east-

ern bluebird, white-eyed vireo, myrtle warbler, meadowlark and towhee.

1, 2   INKBERRY (*Ilex blabra*)

An evergreen shrub growing to six or seven feet. Fruit excellent for birds because it hangs all winter. Requires well-drained soil and open shade.

Eaten by many birds such as the brown thrasher, thrushes, quail and mockingbird.

1, 2, 8   LAUREL (*Kalmia latifolia; K. Angustifolia; K. palifolia;* others)

Very attractive, large-leaved, evergreen shrub with beautiful flowers.

Not important as food, but excellent for cover and nesting sites for many birds.

1, 2, 3,   EUROPEAN PRIVET (*Ligustrum vulgare*)
4, 5, 6,   A common hedge shrub that stands up well in cities
7, 8, 9   and in poor soils.

Provides excellent cover, nesting sites and food for many birds.

2, 3   BEAUTYBERRY (*Callicarpa americana*)
*   Also called French mulberry, this shrub attracts many birds and may save cultivated fruits. Requires rich soil.

Eaten by robin, thrasher, mockingbird and others.

2, 3   SUPPLEJACK (*Berchemia scandens*)
*   A high climbing vine with small greenish-white flowers. Prefers damp soil.

Fruit eaten by thrushes, mockingbird and robin.

8   WAX MYRTLE (*Myrica californica*)

A shrubby tree that prefers dry, sandy soil, similar to bayberry in the east.

Fruit eaten by Audubon's warbler, tree swallow, chickadees and quail.

2, 3   POSSUMHAW (*Ilex decidua*)

Shrubby tree that requires moist, rich soil. Shiny leaves. Reddish fruit.

Eaten by several birds.

8, 9   SALMONBERRY (*Rubus spectabilis*)

In raspberry and blackberry family. Orange-red fruit.

Eaten by grosbeaks, oriole, sparrows, thrushes and jay.

5, 7, 8,   TWINBERRY (*Lonicera involucrata*)
9   Shrub to six feet tall. In honeysuckle family. Requires rich soil and semi-shade.

Fruit eaten by waxwings, grosbeaks, towhee and thrushes.

1   BUCKTHORN (*Rhamnus cathartica*)

Introduced from Europe, this shrub is used for hedges and fence rows. Provides good shelter and nesting sites.

Fruit attracts robins, starlings and other birds from cultivated fruits.

1, 2, 3,   STAGHORN SUMAC (*Rhus typhina*)
4 *   An easily grown shrubby tree that will grow in very poor soil. Reddish fruit lasts all winter. Eaten by at least ninety birds, including ruffed grouse, bobwhite, valley quail, northern and red-shafted flickers, red-bellied and downy woodpeckers,

phoebe, black-capped and Carolina chickadees, wren-tit, Carolina wren, mockingbird, catbird, brown and California thrashers, robin, hermit thrush, eastern bluebird, white-eyed vireo, towhee, Audubon's warbler, goldfinch, and golden-crowned sparrow.

1, 9   YEW (*Taxus canadensis*)
A shrubby plant that is easy to grow in light moist soil. Will grow in shade. Evergreen, with red fruit. Provides excellent cover and nesting sites.
Eaten by several birds.

6, 7, 8,   MANZANITA (*Arctostaphylos nevadensis*)
9 *   Shrubby evergreen with white flowers and red fruit. Good for cover.
Eaten by more than thirty birds including dusky and ruffed grouse, valley and mountain quail, wren-tit and fox sparrow.

Trees

1, 2, 3,   ALDER (*Alnus incana; A. rugosa*)
4   Small tree or shrub, generally preferring moist soil, along banks of streams. In thickets, provides good cover and nesting sites.
Eaten by game birds chiefly, and finches.

9   WESTERN ALDER (*Alnus rubra*)
Tree growing to fifty feet.
Attractive to several birds, among them finches and ducks.

1   ARBORVITAE (*Thuja occidentalis*)
An evergreen growing to fifty feet or more, pre-

ferring moist soil and cool climate. Provides good cover and nesting sites. Easily grown.

Eaten by pine siskins and thrushes.

1 ASH, WHITE (*Fraxinus Americana*)

A large growing tree, generally requiring rich, moist soil. Good tree for yard under these conditions.

Eaten chiefly by finches.

1 BEECH (*Fagus grandifolia*)

Large growing, spreading tree preferring rich, acid soil. Light gray bark, attractive in yard. Fruit, a nut.

Eaten by quail, jay, woodpeckers and woodducks.

1 BIRCH (*Betula lenta; B. populifolia; B. lutea*)

Easily grown, medium sized trees, attractive for planting in yard, especially gray birch (*B. populifolia*).

Fruit eaten by many birds, chiefly finches, blue jay, pheasants, grouse and quail. Attractive to insects which in turn attract many birds.

1, 8, 9 CHERRY, CHOKE (*Prunus virginiana*)
CHERRY, BLACK (*P. seratina*)
CHERRY, RED (*P. pennsylvanica*)

Easily grown, medium sized trees that are attractive in garden. They attract birds from cultivated fruits. Attractive to insects which birds eat. Choke cherry is one of the best garden trees for birds.

Fruit eaten by many birds, especially cedar waxwing, thrushes, finches, catbirds.

1, 2 FLOWERING DOGWOOD (*Cornus florida*)

Small tree with beautiful flowers and red fruit. Easily grown in yard or garden, and is one of the best for landscaping and for birds. Provides nesting sites and excellent food.

Fruit eaten by more than ninety birds, especially thrushes, finches, thrashers and grouse.

1 BALSAM FIR (*Abies balsamea*)
Small growing evergreen that provides good cover. Requires cool climate and good soil.
Eaten by crossbills, chickadees, grouse and jay.

1, 2, 3, HACKBERRY (*Celtis occidentalis*)
4, 5, 6, Medium sized tree that prefers dry, rich soil. Pro-
7, 8, 9 vides fair cover and nesting sites, but excellent food.
* Eaten by forty or more species of birds, including flicker, yellow-bellied sapsucker, mockingbird, brown thrasher, robin, eastern bluebird, cedar waxwing, cardinal.

1, 9 HEMLOCK (*Tsuga canadensis*)
Evergreen, attractive for planting as tree or hedge. Requires light, moist soil. Provides very good cover and good nesting sites and food.
Eaten by winter finches chiefly, such as crossbills and siskins.

1, 2, 3, HAWTHORN (*Crataegus crusgalli*)
4, 5, 6, THICKET THORN (*C. Coccinea*)
7, 8, 9 COCKSPURTHORN (*C. Cordata*)
* Shrubby trees with large fruit. Thorns make it good for fences or hedges. Requires good soil and sun. Provides good cover and nesting sites.
Eaten by thirty-nine kinds of birds, including grouse, robin, pine grosbeak and purple finch.

1, 2   MAPLE (*Acer rubrum; A. saccharinum*)
Easily grown, attractive trees for yard or garden.
Provide fair cover and nesting sites.
Eaten by several birds, including cardinal and pine
grosbeaks.

1, 4, 5,   MOUNTAIN ASH (*Sorbus americana*)
6, 7, 9   Medium sized tree, easily grown, requiring a good
  *   moist soil. Reddish fruit attractive to birds during
fall and winter months.
Eaten by fifteen species of birds, among them being
the red-headed woodpecker, catbird, brown
thrasher, robin, Bohemian and cedar waxwings,
Baltimore oriole, evening and pine grosbeaks.

1, 2, 3,   MULBERRY (*Morus rubra*)
4, 6 *   Medium sized, spreading tree, easily grown in good
soil. Except for messy fruit, attractive for yard
plantings. Fruit attracts birds from cultivated fruit
trees. Eaten by sixty kinds of birds, including yellow-billed cuckoo, red-bellied, red-headed and
downy woodpeckers, eastern kingbird, mockingbird, catbird and robin, wood thrush, cedar waxwing, red-eyed vireo, yellow warbler, orchard and
Baltimore orioles, scarlet tanager, and purple finch.

1   OAK (*Quercus alba; Q. borealis*)
Large trees, requiring good soil. Foliage nice in fall.
Good trees for yard or garden. Attract insects
which attract warblers in spring.
Eaten by many birds, including pheasants, grouse,
finches, blue jay, thrasher, woodduck, thrushes, and
woodpeckers.

1, 2, 9 PINE, NORWAY (*Pinus resinosa*)
PINE, WHITE (*Pinus stroba*)
PINE, AUSTRIAN (*Pinus nigra*)
Large growing evergreens, very attractive for garden plantings. Provides good cover, nesting sites, and food. Easily grown in most places. Austrian pine good for city planting. Used for nesting by purple finch, siskin and several warblers.
Eaten by many birds, chiefly crossbills, siskins, woodpeckers, nuthatches, chickadees and waxwings.

1, 2, 4, RED CEDAR (*Juniperus virginiana*; others)
5, 6, 7, An easily grown evergreen that prefers dry soil and
8, 9 * sun. Provides excellant cover, nesting sites and winter food. Makes a good hedge or fence row, or background for yard or garden.
Eaten by fifty kinds of birds, among them being the flicker, mockingbird, robin, eastern bluebird, cedar waxwing, myrtle warbler, evening and pine grosbeaks, and purple finch.

1, 2, 3 SASSAFRAS (*Sassafras variifolium*)
* A good tree for yard or garden, with attractive yellowish flowers in early spring, and nice fall foliage. Easy to grow in any soil. Provides good cover and nesting sites.
Eaten by eighteen kinds of birds, including bobwhite, eastern kingbird, catbird, robin, veery and red-eyed vireo.

1, 2, 4, SHADBUSH (*Amelanchier canadensis*; others)
6, 7, 9 A shrubby tree, easy to grow, with attractive, white

flowers and dark red fruit. Will grow in any soil. Provides fair cover and nesting sites, but is one of the best plants for food for birds.

Eaten by forty-two kinds of birds among them being the flicker, catbird, robin, hermit thrush, veery, cedar waxwing and Baltimore oriole.

1, 2, 3
*
Sour Gum (*Tupelo*) (*Nyssa sylvatica*)

An attractive garden tree for foliage in fall. Prefers heavy, moist soil. Provides good cover and nesting sites. Easy to grow.

Eaten by thirty-nine kinds of birds, including the flicker, robin, olive-backed and gray-cheeked thrushes, cedar waxwing and purple finch.

1, 2, 4,
5, 7, 8,
9
Spruce, White (*Picea canadensis*)
Spruce, Norway (*Picea excelsa*; others)

Attractive evergreens that generally require a good soil. Easily grown and make good windbreaks and naturalistic plantings. Provides good cover and nesting sites.

Eaten by winter finches, chickadees and thrushes.

1, 2
Flowering Crab (*Malus floribunda*)

A very attractive small tree with beautiful flowers and nice fall foliage. Provides good cover and nesting sites.

Eaten by many birds, especially mockingbirds, thrasher and catbird.

1, 2, 3,
4, 5, 6,
7, 8, 9
Willow (*Salix*- many varieties)

Shrubby trees to large trees. Select a variety native to locality. Easy to grow and attractive in garden. Attractive to birds because of insects on leaves.

Fruit eaten by several birds including grosbeaks.

1   EUROPEAN LARCH (*Larix decidera europeus*)
Resembling an evergreen, but leaves drop off in winter. Will grow in any good moist soil. Nice tree for garden planting.
Buds eaten by many birds in spring. Also attractive to birds because of insects on it.

1, 2, 3   PERSIMMON (*Diospyros virginiana*)
Medium sized tree, requiring good soil. Large, yellowish fruit. Provides fair cover and nesting sites.
Eaten by several kinds of birds.

2, 3   SWEETBAY (*Persea pubescens*)
Small tree, requiring moist soil. Evergreen, with bluish-black fruit. Provides good cover and nesting sites.
Eaten by robin and other birds in winter.

3, 6   IRONWOOD, BLACK (*Krugiodendron ferreum*)
Evergreen shrub with cherry-like fruit. Good for cover and nesting sites.
Eaten by thrasher, mockingbird and oriole.

8, 9   CASCARA (*Rhomus purshiana*)
A shrub or small tree, occasionally forty feet high. Grows best in rich soil.
Fruit eaten by thrashers, thrushes and jays.

6, 7, 8, 9   MADROÑA (*Arbutus menziesi*)
A large, evergreen tree, with wide leathery leaves. Clusters of white flowers, and a reddish-orange fruit.
Eaten by solitaire, waxwing, doves, flicker and robin.

8, 9   MAPLE, BIGLEAF (*Acer macrophyllum*)
        MAPLE, DWARF (*A. glabrum*)
        Medium sized trees, attractive in plantings. Provide
        good cover and nesting sites.
        Eaten by finches and many other birds.

1, 2, 4,   APPLE (*Malus*- many varieties)
5, 7, 9   Easily grown fruit tree, requiring sun and good soil.
    *   Provides cover and nesting sites for many birds,
        especially in group plantings. Attracts insects which
        attract birds.
        Fruit eaten by ruffed grouse, ring-necked pheasant,
        mockingbird, robin, cedar waxwing, purple finch,
        pine grosbeak and red crossbill.

Plants to Attract Hummingbirds

Although hummingbirds will feed on the blossoms of many
of the plants in the above list, they generally prefer flowers
with orange or reddish blossoms.

Thus the flowers of such garden favorites as azalea, colum-
bine, delphinium, phlox, geranium, fuchsia, cardinal flower,
tiger lily, morning glories, scarlet runner bean, petunias,
hollyhocks, beebalms, and others will prove attractive to
those interesting little birds. A clump of jewel weed (touch-
me-not) near our place is always the center of attraction for
hummers from the time the plants first bloom. Flowering
raspberry has also been seen to be popular with these birds.

Plants to Attract Ducks

Many ponds or lakes, either natural or artificial, may be of
the type that can be made more attractive to ducks. Many

times, all that is required is the introduction of certain food plants. If there is a pond or lake in which you can make such plantings nearby, and if you are interested in the idea, first get in touch with the Fish and Wildlife Service, Washington, D. C.

A questionnaire will be sent, the results of which will enable the experts to suggest the plants that will grow in the water. You will probably have to send specimens of plants already growing there, soil specimens and water samples, for only by analysis of these samples can reliable suggestions be made.

Some of the plants that may be recommended are wild millet and some of the smartweeds for the marshy areas around the lake, and long-leaf pondweed, and duckweeds for the lake itself. A list of the dealers in duck-food plants can be obtained from the same Fish and Wildlife Service.

CHAPTER *5*

BIRDS IN WINTER

In many respects winter is the most interesting season for back yard birding. The chief activity of birds during the cold weather is finding enough food to maintain their body heat, and thus keep alive. Consequently, a variety of feeders in the yard will attract birds of many different kinds and frequently in large numbers. Some of the winter visitors are quite colorful, despite their winter plumage, and this color and movement in the garden can almost take the place of summer greenery and blooms.

But probably the most interesting thing about birds in winter is the ease with which they may be tamed. Later on, as they build their nests and raise their broods of young, they have more fear of man and may be more difficult to watch closely. In winter, though, it is not uncommon to get several species of birds to eat from your hand, or at least to come within a very few feet of you for food.

It takes patience and sometimes long hours of sitting quietly in one position, but it can be done if you try hard enough.

Blue jays are probably the easiest birds to start with, because they are naturally bold, and are reasonably common in most places. We have four that use our feeders daily, and recently we tried to tame them. We knew that they liked peanuts, so we used ordinary roasted peanuts in the shell, for bait.

On the sill of a south window, we have a simple tray feeder. Jays had become accustomed to feeding there. In fact, within an hour after we nailed it up, the four jays had come to eat peanuts and sunflower seed. So, one Saturday morning when we had plenty of time, we started our experiment.

We put out three peanuts for the four jays. One jay went without a peanut and flew off to the maple to scream his displeasure. We opened the window over the feeder, and set out three more peanuts on the sill. Again one jay went without a peanut. The next time we placed three peanuts on the inside of the window on the sill.

This time the jays were more wary, but finally they came in for the food. Inside the room is a bookcase, the top of which is at the windowsill level, so the fourth batch of peanuts was placed on the bookcase. In ten minutes or so the jays were daring enough to enter the house, snatch a peanut and fly away. We continued the process, moving the peanuts further and further into the room, until the jays were flying through the window, perching on a table, and eating peanuts. The whole experiment took less than an hour.

Requiring considerably more time, and resulting in much more fun, were the experiments of Dr. Frederick Brooks and Maurice Brooks of Morgantown, West Virginia. They were successful in getting ten species of birds to eat from their hands—tufted titmouse, Carolina chickadee, white-breasted nuthatch, Carolina wren, downy woodpecker, junco, tree sparrow, white-throated sparrow, cardinal and red-bellied woodpecker.

Their method was a novel one and easy for anyone who has the patience to try it.

The first part of the plan consisted of making an artificial arm out of a stick, and clothing it with a sleeve and glove. Dr. Brooks placed the "arm" out of his library window so that it extended across the feeding tray. He placed a few walnut meats in the open palm of the artificial hand. Birds very soon found the food and lost all fear of this new fangled feeder.

Then one day, he removed the wooden arm, and stuck his own out the window. He wore a glove at first and held nutmeats in his hand. The birds came and fed as before. The next step was to take off the glove and let the nuthatches, titmice, juncos, wrens and woodpeckers hang on his bare fingers while they pecked away at the food.

But he wanted to carry out the idea still further, so he made a crude dummy out of a post, a gourd for a head, some old clothing and a hat. He even placed a corncob pipe in the mouth.

Nutmeats and seeds were scattered on the crown of the hat, in the pipe and on the outstretched arm and hand. The birds were wary at first, but soon became accustomed to the dummy standing in one place for several days. The titmice and juncos were the first to become bold enough to perch on the hat, hand and pipe. Soon after other birds lost their fear of this "man" and came to feed.

Dr. Brooks' next step was to move the dummy and stand in its place, in the same position. The result was as expected. The birds ate off the top of his head, out of his pipe, and off his arm and hand. It took time, but the birds did become tame.

One of the strangest sights we ever saw, and one that we would not have believed if we had not seen it ourselves, was at the pond where our friend played host to a thousand or so ducks every day during the winter. His pond was about a mile from a large reservoir upon which thousands of ducks spent the winter. Some of the birds would shuttle back and forth between pond and reservoir to feed on the pond, and rest in the center of the larger body of water. Some of the birds had become quite tame and would come when called— all the way from the reservoir to the pond.

One afternoon we had planned to visit the pond and take photographs of the ducks feeding there. But upon arrival, there was not a duck to be found. We hunted up the care-taker and asked what had happened. He told us not to worry, that he would call the ducks over, and we could take all the pictures we wanted. We must have looked a little bewildered, because he laughed and told us to get the camera set up and ready to shoot. We would have ducks in ten minutes.

He filled two pails with cracked corn and walked down to the edge of the pond. When we were hidden in the blind, he started his calling, and frankly, we thought he was a candidate for a strait jacket. No imitation duck-call rang out through the winter air. Instead, he shouted out, "Here ducky, here, ducky, here, ducky," as one would call a pet poodle. We started to put up the camera when we heard the first quacks in the distance. In a minute or two, eight or ten black ducks dropped in over the oaks and splashed into the pond.

The next ten minutes was nothing but focus and shoot, focus and shoot, change film packs, focus and shoot. Ducks came in by the hundreds, until close to a thousand were splashing around after corn. Some even went up on the lawn to eat out of his hand.

The next day, we asked him to repeat the calling act, but this time, we wanted to be at the reservoir. We set a time, and at that time, we listened and watched. Not a sound could we hear, and for no apparent reason, eight ducks jumped from the reservoir and headed for the pond. A dozen more followed, then fifty more. In a minute or two there was a black line of ducks headed straight for the small pond a half-mile away. We had deliberately set the time an hour earlier, so we feel sure it was not a time pattern that caused the ducks to go to feed. They must have heard the call and associated it with food—for away they went.

Before any attempt may be made to tame the birds in the yard, first the birds must be attracted to the garden and become accustomed to finding food there. Generally speaking, there are two types of food to put out—seeds for birds such as sparrows, juncos and grosbeaks; and suet or other fat for insect-eating birds such as woodpeckers, nuthatches and brown creepers.

As a start, two or three simple feeders may be used both to find out which birds may be attracted and what these birds prefer to eat in your locality.

The simplest kind of a suet holder is a ten-cent store metal

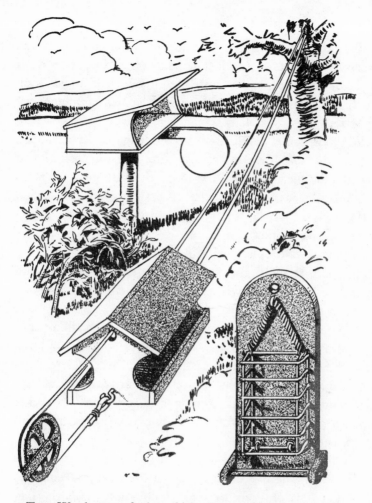

Top—Weathervane feeder which protects food from rain or snow and assures birds of a sheltered spot to feed.

Lower left—Trolley feeder for wary birds. Start at tree and after birds start to use it, move feeder a foot closer to house every few days, until birds are feeding off the windowsill.

Lower right—A simple suet rack made from a ten-cent-store soap dish. Hang it on a tree trunk or post.

soap dish, the kind that has a spring on each end to stretch between the faucets of the kitchen sink. The soap dish itself is made of strips of heavy wire, from one half to an inch apart. If the strips are less than an inch apart, cut out every other strip.

Next, melt some paraffin in an old pan, or in a tincan, and dunk the soap dish in the paraffin. The purpose of this job is to coat the metal with wax. If the weather gets very cold before the fat from the suet covers the metal, the metal may be so cold that the soft parts of birds will freeze to it—their eyes, bills, or feet.

Next, drive two small nails in a tree or clothespost, far enough apart to hold the soap dish when the springs are stretched. Fill the dish with suet scraps, and wait and see what happens.

Another simple suet holder may be made by drilling several half-inch holes in a piece of wood, a foot or so long, such as the lower end of a Christmas tree. Push suet or even peanut butter into the holes. Fasten a screw-eye in one end of the wood, and hang it from a tree, or from a bracket fastened to a post. Nuthatches and chickadees generally will use such a feeding device.

A third easy way is to use a wide mesh bag, such as oranges come in. Wash the bag out to remove the dye, and cut it in half so that it is only six or eight inches long. Fill the bag with suet, and pull the open ends together and twist them several times to force some of the suet out through the mesh. Then, tie a string to the top, and hang it in a tree.

The simplest sort of a seed tray is a board about two feet long and ten or twelve inches wide, with an edging an inch

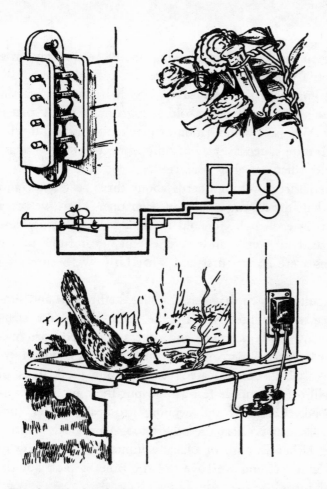

Top left—A dowel-stick suet holder is a fine "junior" craft project and will attract many birds.

Top right—A tube of sugar syrup attached to shrubbery may attract hummingbirds to the garden.

Bottom—Some birds sneak up and feed without attracting much attention. A doorbell "trap" will warn of their arrival. The only equipment required is a doorbell buzzer, two dry cells, and some wire.

high to keep the seeds from blowing off. Place the tray on a post, or on a windowsill, four or five feet off the ground.

Scatter commercial wild bird seed on it if you can get it. If not, the seed combinations sold as pigeon feed may prove attractive. We use a combination of chicken scratch and wild bird food quite successfully, but only after a test some years ago to find what the birds preferred.

We used three or four boards about three feet long, and drilled a half-dozen large holes in each one. Then we set a paper cup in each hole, to hold the seed. We put only one kind of seed in a cup, and watched them carefully to see what cups were empty first and what birds were emptying the cups.

The results showed that hemp, millet, kaffir corn and sunflower seeds were preferred by the wild birds—tree sparrows, juncos, field sparrows, and others. Cracked corn was preferred by house sparrows, cowbirds and jays, which are almost classed as domesticated birds in our yard. Jays of course will eat peanuts as fast as you put them out, and sunflower seeds. Cardinals and evening grosbeaks prefer sunflower seeds, but will eat the others too. Most birds will eat nutmeats, either English or black walnuts, but somehow or other so will we, and we have not the time to pick out the meats for birds.

Many birds, in fact most of the birds that visit feeders, are quite cosmopolitan in their tastes. You may have to experiment for a while to see what they prefer, but once they start coming they will eat a great variety of foods.

We have seen wintering brown thrashers on Long Island that really went for toasted whole-wheat breadcrumbs, made after the bread was buttered. They would eat scarcely anything else at the feeder, but they certainly gobbled up those crumbs.

We have read recently of catbirds that showed a remarkable fondness for cheese, bread, raisins, currants, milk, corn flakes, puffed wheat soaked in milk, mushrooms, boiled potatoes, fried fish, beef stew and beef soup. Of course, all birds do not go to this extreme, but occasionally one turns up that will eat almost anything.

Raisins, currants, bits of apple, pieces of banana and other fruit are readily eaten by most birds, but especially thrashers, thrushes and robins. Even woodpeckers, red-heads particularly, will go for such food. California thrashers have been described as being fond of figs, seedless grapes, pomegranates and other fruit cut up in small pieces.

Chickadees are notorious lovers of doughnuts, either crumbled on a feeder, or hung by a string from a tree. We have seen photographs of a feeder in which several nails had been driven, with the points upward. Every day doughnuts were impaled on the nails, and chickadees cleaned them up each day.

We attracted a large flock of red-wings to our yard by throwing out left-over turkey dressing. The red-wings had been perching in the maple for a few minutes each day, but they refused to come down to the feeders. But when they discovered the turkey dressing they came to stay. Every day for the rest of the winter they came in a flock of a hundred or more to eat the same millet, hemp and corn as the other birds. We could not feed them turkey dressing every day, but they got it a few more times.

Another stunt that attracts birds is to collect berries in the fall, dry them, and save them till the snow falls. Then birds will flock to bayberry, viburnum, sumac, elder, and other wild fruits. We have seen myrtle warblers, cedar waxwings, and wintering robins feeding at window feeders on these dried fruits.

If at first birds will not use the feeders put out for them, there are one or two tricks to try. First, try putting out suet and seeds in more natural situations than in man-made feeders. Tie pieces of suet to trunks and branches of trees, or push suet into the cracks in the bark. Melt suet and pour it down the side of a tree or post. Try using other kinds of meat fat, bacon or ham fat, or even left-over kitchen fat. Grind it up in a meat chopper, cut it up into small pieces with a knife, and scatter it on the lawn, or under the shrubs some distance from the house.

Be sure to tie suet on trees securely, otherwise one bird may carry away an entire piece. Squirrels, too, will make short work of suet that is easily carried away. Probably the easiest way is to place a piece of suet on a small branch, and wrap a piece of string around it several times.

In the same way, seeds and nuts may be scattered on the ground some distance from the house. The only danger in this practice though, is that a cat may hide in nearby shrubbery to pounce on birds as they feed. Then too, when it rains or snows, the feed will become soaked or covered up.

Natural looking feeders frequently will attract birds when no other device will. A piece of log rotted out or hollowed out may be filled with seed, nuts, suet scraps, breadcrumbs and other feed, and placed in a likely spot. Another attractive feeder may be made by using a board, or two boards nailed together, to give you a base eighteen inches or two feet square.

In each corner of the base drill a hole, and in each hole stick a small sapling or branch, an inch in diameter and three feet long. Then bend the branches over so that they come together on top, tepee fashion. Tie them together.

Then cut some branches from one of the evergreens— spruce, cedar, yew or pine—and weave them through the uprights so you get a roof effect. Of course, leave one side open. Hang these feeders from a tree, or place them on a pole. Fill them with seed, and place some suet scraps and seeds in the evergreen branches themselves. This type of feeder is more natural looking, but better yet, it has a top that will keep rain and snow from soaking or covering the feed.

A very successful stunt for getting birds to feed near the house is to build a "trolley feeder." Use any kind of a box with a floor, roof, and open sides. Fasten two pulleys on the top. Then hang the feeder on a long wire, extending from the house to a tree or pole some distance away. When birds become accustomed to feeding there, move the feeder a foot or two closer to the house. A few days later, move it again. Finally, after several days, or two weeks, the birds should be eating from the windowsill.

As time goes on, and birds are attracted to your yard, you may want more elaborate feeders, built to last for many years. Again, there are many good feeders to be found in department stores, seed stores, or garden supply shops. The National Audubon Society in New York sells a nice variety of feeders, and will send a descriptive list upon request.

If you prefer making your own, the drawings on these

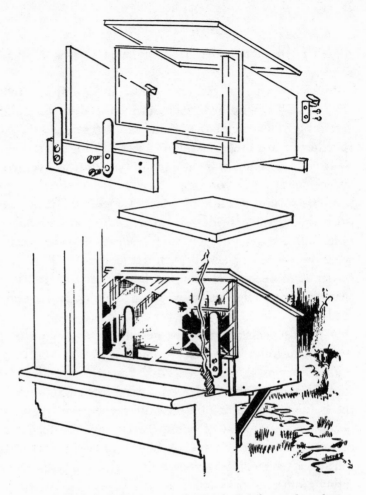

Many birds will flock to a window feeder for seeds and suet. A wood and glass feeder such as this is fun to make and more fun to watch, as jays, juncos, chickadees, cardinals or grosbeaks visit it daily.

pages will supply ideas. The window feeder on page 132 is especially recommended as a good sturdy type that has several advantages. The glass top and back afford a good view of what is going on inside and at the same time will keep off rain and wind. Seeds may be scattered on the bottom, or placed in racks along one side. A suet rack may be placed on the other side to attract chickadees, nuthatches and downy woodpeckers.

A large weathervane feeder for the lawn is also desirable, if it is easily seen from the window. Swinging with the wind, birds will always have shelter from the weather, and feed on the inside will be protected. A pipe pole is preferred if possible, since cats and squirrels have difficulty climbing it.

With such a variety of feeders, and with a variety of food to attract different species of birds, there are few places where at least a few birds cannot be induced to feed regularly. But once feeding has been started, continue it all winter. Birds come to rely on it, and without it they may die.

If you start early enough in the fall, it is possible to get several migratory birds to winter over, or at least to stay beyond their usual time for moving south. Other birds which usually winter in marshes or deep woods where the food supply may be greater, instead may winter in and around your garden.

Thus it is that robins, bluebirds, brown thrashers, hermit thrushes, catbirds, myrtle warblers and other birds which are usually thought of as spring and summer birds in the northeast, have now become reasonably common in winter around places where feeding stations are kept up from fall until spring. In some cases these birds feed almost entirely on the fruit of plants in the garden. In other cases they visit feeders too. It certainly would be a mean trick to entice these birds into staying all winter, and then because it was not convenient, or because the snow was too deep, or the weather too cold, to stop feeding them even for a day.

Birds can withstand cold weather if they have plenty of food to produce body heat, and if they find some degree of shelter from the cold. That is why many of them eat fats, and fatty seeds. These foods will produce the heat necessary to keep them alive.

Another general rule is to set out the feed at night, or late afternoon. Many birds are early feeders and will visit the yard even before sunrise. If they find no food then they may lose the habit of coming there. However, you may have an experience similar to ours that makes that practice difficult.

We had just started our fall feeding program and were getting into the habit of filling the feeders at night when we aired the dog. We would scatter the seeds and place the peanuts for the jays on the window feeders and lawn feeders at about ten or ten-thirty every night. In fact, we were just becoming accustomed to the early morning screams of the jays and had succeeded in sleeping through them.

Then, one morning we were going on a hunting trip and had arisen about four-thirty. We casually glanced at the window feeders—and stopped in surprise. We looked again. No peanuts. Half of the other feed was gone too. That particular feeder was on a second floor window, and we began to wonder. Birds feed only during the day, or so we thought. Squirrels feed during the day. But what took the feed at night?

Our problem bothered us for the several days we were away. When we returned home, we found the same thing had been going on, and the jays had about deserted us. We decided to set a camera trap so that whatever was eating between eleven at night and six in the morning would take its own picture.

That night we set the trap, baited with peanuts. Not more than twenty minutes later—flash, off went the bulb, and we had one picture of our midnight visitors. We baited the trap again and reset the camera. Ten minutes later we had another picture. The next time we set out bait and sat close beside the window to watch. We soon had our answer.

Half a dozen deermice appeared from the ivy vines on the house, and swarmed over the feeder. They went first for the peanuts, then for the sunflower seeds. The corn went next, and after that the smaller seeds.

We tried trapping a few of the mice and we caught a dozen or more, but the supply seemed unlimited. Our solution was to put out the feed the first thing in the morning and hope for the best. Fortunately, the jays changed their feeding habits.

We have even changed some of our habits so as to get in ten minutes of birding every morning. Our present schedule calls for catching a 7:41 train every morning, which means getting up at six-thirty when it is still dark. As it starts to get light about six forty-five to seven, the birds start to arrive at the feeder, and we have found that by using an electric razor we may shave and watch birds at the same time. We can eat breakfast and watch them, which we do. But the shaving trick has added ten minutes a day to our bird watching. The only disadvantage is that an unusual bird may cause us to leave one side unshaven or to catch the 8:04. But that does not happen very often. The only problem we have not solved is how to hold binoculars while shaving. The vibration of the razor causes the birds to jump up and down at too many vibrations per minute to make sure identification possible. Perhaps some bird-loving razor manufacturer can help us.

Some of our bird-watching friends accuse us of overdoing it a little. But the number of different birds seen in the yard is in direct proportion to the number of hours spent watching. The more time spent, the more birds you see. You cannot always rely on interesting birds to arrive on Saturday or Sunday. Some of them may prefer weekdays.

Once you get birds to visit your yard regularly, there are all sorts of interesting things to do. Some of them may be used to astound your friends, something like card tricks or magic acts. Some of your friends may doubt your sanity, but do not let that worry you. A bird-watching hobby is certainly as wholesome as batting a little round ball around an open field full of sand holes, or hitting a slightly larger ball back and forth on some sun-baked clay. Some people do have their doubts about birders though, like the worried mother who one day walked into the Audubon Society office.

Talking with the editor of the *Audubon Magazine*, she beat around the bush for several minutes, then got to the point of her visit. It seemed that her fourteen-year-old son had become interested in birds to the complete exclusion of more manly hobbies such as football and baseball. She was worried about the type of man her son might meet if he continued his hobby, and she wondered if she might see a real professional ornithologist. Were they real, virile he-men, or were they, er, ah, you know . . . !

The Audubon editor, at that point engaged to a former intercollegiate running champion and more recently one of this country's better-known field ornithologists (and author of *Guide to Bird Watching*, page 200), assured the mother of the virility of most male birders. She listed a few of the better-known ornithologists, all of whom were happily married and doing an adequate job of providing future naturalists. Very much relieved, the mother left.

The story should have a more happy ending, that the boy went on to be a brilliant ornithologist. But that was the last we ever heard of him.

One friend of ours listened to blue jays and practiced their call. She waited till the youngsters were in school, and her husband blissfully on his way to the office. Then she would do the house work to the accompaniment of her own blue jay screams. When she had it perfected, she tried it out in the yard where neighbors could not see her, and soon had jays coming to her call. She then threw them a handful of peanuts, and went back in the house.

One day she decided she would make her debut in public. A few friends were there for tea, and the winter afternoon being quite warm, they walked around the garden. Off in the distance a jay was heard. Our friend answered. Her friends jumped a foot, and looked around the ground and up in the tree. No jay. They could not believe the sound came from their peaceful sane-looking hostess. But it happened again, and they were on the point of taking a hurried departure. Two jays came just then, and perched in the tree. Our friend took some peanuts from her pocket and held them up. Down came a jay, picked one out of her hand, and flew back to the tree. Down came the second jay. Nonchalantly she tossed the rest of the peanuts on the ground and invited her guests to tea.

A man that we read of recently had a similar stunt involving a downy woodpecker. One downy visited his suet holder regularly and he found that he could stand some ten feet away, and throw a walnut meat into the air. Before it touched the ground, the downy would swoop down and snatch it, and return to perch where he would peck at it until it was gone. We have tried that trick but a squirrel or blue jay always beat the downy to the nut. Someday, maybe we can get the downy alone.

Our flock of English sparrows though, does provide amusement on occasion. They are now accustomed to eat on the windowsill, and most of the time they find an ample supply. However, once in a while we overlook that one feeder, but the sparrows soon let us know of our failure. They line up on the sill, stretch up the four inches or so necessary to reach the glass, and bang away with their bills for all they are worth. If we do not immediately put out some food, they continue the rapping until we do. When we open the window they fly to a perch in the hydrangea and the second the window goes down, back they come.

One winter we had quite a bit of fun with a white-breasted nuthatch. Observation over several days showed that the bird came only at four o'clock every day to the suet holder just outside the window. Rarely was it more than a few minutes off. We used that knowledge to have fun with a few friends

who knew nothing about birds. As we sat talking, the con-
versation inevitably got to birds, and just as surely came the
question, "What kind of birds come to your yard?"

We would list the usual birds—some eight or ten of them,
using an occasional Latin name to make a common bird sound
quite unusual. Then we would glance quite casually at our
watch, and say "M-m! Four o'clock! Want to see a white-
breasted nuthatch?" The answer was always, "Yes, but what
has four o'clock got to do with it?" We would then explain
that this bird came every day, precisely at four. It was just
a commonplace statement to us, but we found that it was
quite unusual to our friends. Imagine a bird being able to tell
time!

We would then explain that telling time had nothing to
do with it, that birds lived according to instinct and certain
behavior patterns based on environment. This bird got in the
habit of coming about that time, and that is all there was to
it. Nothing unusual. But our friends still insisted that we had
quite an unusual bird.

If some of your friends are like some of ours, you can build
quite a reputation for having remarkable eyesight. Just glance
at a downy woodpecker out on the tree and make a casual
remark as to its sex. Usually, the question will be asked,
"How do you know?"

Pass over the binoculars, and say, "Take a look—it is perfectly obvious. Can you not tell?" Rather than admit they
cannot quite see how you tell, the answer always is, "Oh,
sure! So it is!"

It is obvious, but not for the reason supposed. A male
downy has a red patch on the back of his head. The female

does not. But not many non-birders know that, and you get credit for superhuman eyesight.

As you watch birds during the winter you are likely to see many interesting habits. One observer told us about a nuthatch that visited his feeder daily. One day as he watched from the window, the nuthatch flew to the windowsill, picked up a seed or two and carried them to an oak, where the seeds were cached in the heavy bark. The nuthatch would then return for another bit of food. But each time the nuthatch left the oak, down came a hairy woodpecker which quickly pecked the seed from the bark and flew back to the top of the oak. This went on for several minutes before the nuthatch saw the woodpecker. It tried a few times more, but the woodpecker got the food each time. The nuthatch ran around the tree, searching apparently for its lost food, then flew off with "yank-yank-yanks" of indignant rage.

We have watched blue jays do about the same thing. One jay would fly to our feeder for peanuts. It would then fly off to a corner of the fence where leaves had been piled up by the wind. It would drop a peanut in the leaves, drop a leaf or two on top, and fly back for another. But each time it left the leaves, another jay flew down, quickly picked around and came up with the peanut. But the first jay was not as docile about the theft as the nuthatch. When it finally discovered the second jay, it screamed in anger and attacked the thieving or playful bird. It finally drove it off, and then came back to hide some more food.

Other observers of birds in winter have seen some interesting attempts of birds seeking shelter for the night. Anyone who lives in a large city has undoubtedly seen starlings roost on public buildings by the thousands. Observations in New York tend to show that starlings come from several miles away to roost in numbers up to fifty thousand, on the coping and ledges of the Metropolitan Museum of Art. In Washington, it is the Treasury Building that provides shelter for roosting starlings, and many other cities have their counterparts.

One observer writes of two brown creepers that clung nightly to the stucco on the front of the house, not more than a foot from the front door. The birds would arrive at dusk, and roost there until dawn, on the flat side of the house. When an attempt was made to give them a more adequate shelter, by nailing up a board under which they might crawl, the birds moved to the other side of the door. When the board was removed, back they came.

Another observer had an equally interesting experience with creepers. On the barn of a neighboring farm was a beam that extended out from one end. The end of the rafter was rotted out so as to form a hollow space a foot or two deep. Eleven creepers were observed flying into the opening at dusk and flying out again early in the morning.

One winter a Carolina wren spent its nights in a studio in Haddonfield, New Jersey. The first night it flew in the open door. In the morning, out it went. But it soon learned to use a small hole in the door, and came and went at will. The bird roosted, ate, drank, bathed and sang there all winter, occasionally flying into the dining-room to pick up crumbs.

One winter we had spent considerable time looking for a saw whet owl. We knew that they usually roosted in evergreens, and we searched every grove within several miles of our home. Long-eared owls were common it seemed, but not a saw whet could we find. We had just about given up the search when one morning we went out to the front steps for the milk, and there on a lower limb of a blue spruce sat a saw whet. We moved slowly so as not to frighten it, but it seemed to be asleep and paid no attention to the clinking of the bottles.

We called the rest of the family to see the bird from the window, and still it perched, not three feet from the house. It was in a sheltered spot, out of the wind, and apparently the heat from the house made it content to stay there. We opened the window, shot flash bulbs off in its face, and never did we have a more obliging model. It opened both eyes and stared. Closed one eye, and cocked its head. Opened that eye and closed the other. It behaved perfectly for half an hour.

Then we approached it more closely. We stood beside the limb, and gently rubbed our finger on the back of the owl's legs. It lifted first one leg and grasped our finger, then the other. Finally, it perched on our hand, and we turned it around for a good look. Ten minutes later, we returned it to the tree where it roosted off and on for several days. With one exception, it was the tamest saw whet we ever saw, and saw whets are notoriously tame in fall and winter.

A friend of ours, a birder, was reading one cold fall night, when he heard a crash against the window. He opened it and there on the sill was a partly-stunned saw whet. He picked it up, brought it inside, and closed the window. That owl became a family pet, and remained there for several years. During the day it perched on the kitchen door, watching every movement in the kitchen. At first, its diet was hamburger and other raw meat, with an occasional drop or two of cod liver oil for vitamins. Finally, the diet was a mouse or two each week, which were obtained from a nearby laboratory. Our friend would whirl the mouse around by its tail till it was a little dizzy, then drop it in the middle of the kitchen floor. The mouse would start to stagger away when down would swoop the owl, snatch it up in its claws, and fly back to the door to eat it. It was not half as gruesome as you might suppose, unless you particularly like mice. The owl was quite neat and clean about its kill, rarely leaving a sign of its meals. It was a lot more tidy than our two children, who seem to get many more crumbs on the floor than they do in their mouths.

Feeding birds in the yard does provide many interesting moments, but it also has its aggravating times. It may not be true of all back yard birders, but it certainly bothers us to spend hours building feeders and then setting them up, only to have a flock of English sparrows and starlings and a couple of squirrels start to clean up the food before we get back into the house. These birds arrive in flocks of a hundred or more, and that many birds can make short work of five pounds of feed. Not only that, but they drive away most other birds, especially the smaller and much more desirable winter birds. We like English sparrows in the summer when they eat beetles; and starlings as they walk around the lawn cleaning up beetle grubs. But we do not care for them in winter as they drive the juncos and tree sparrows from the feeder; or in the case of starlings, as they drive the downies and nuthatches from the suet rack.

A few experiments, based on suggestions of other birders, have shown us a way out. It may not work everywhere, but it works in our yard. We have found that hanging feeders that sway in the wind will discourage these birds—especially if there are no perches for them to cling to while they feed. Most of the other birds can cling to feeders and get all the suet or seeds they need. But most of the sparrows cannot or will not use hanging feeders, so we rigged up a tray on the clothespost for them.

One end of the tray is fastened to the post with a hinge. It tends to drop, without a support at the other end. The support is a piece of string running from the top of the post to a light spring which is attached to the tray. Thus, when a bird lights on the tray, it bobs up and down. English sparrows being more wary, will avoid this feeder. But the more desirable birds use it regularly.

Our weathervane feeder, which stands some five feet from the ground, also is avoided by English sparrows and starlings. This feeder swings in the wind and apparently the movement frightens off the undesirable birds. We do provide food for those birds, but chiefly to bait them from the other feeders. We mounted a feeder on an old stump, and keep it stocked with chicken scratch and suet. The English sparrows and starlings flock there, and leave the other feeders closer to the house for the birds we want to see more closely.

Squirrels are a little more difficult to control. In fact, we have come to the conclusion that traps, or an air rifle are the best controls. Hanging feeders, with a large inverted-cone roof may keep squirrels from getting at the seed. But there cannot be a nearby branch from which a squirrel can jump to the feeder and get in under the top. Sheet aluminum, sheet tin, or other metal may be made into a guard for poles upon which feeders are placed. But they must be high enough so that squirrels cannot jump over them. The feeders must be far enough from trees so that squirrels cannot jump from outreaching branches.

The best kind of a guard seems to be a conical or lamp-shade-shaped piece of metal that fits tightly around the post, and extends out at least fifteen inches all around. It should be six or seven feet from the ground. A method that has also worked, is to wrap barbed wire around the pole in a dense mass, about twelve inches wide, and four or five feet from the ground. Unfortunately, the barbed wire may be as hard on you as on the squirrel. But if there are squirrels in your vicinity, your bird feeding program will soon attract them. And one squirrel can eat the food of many birds, and while it is feeding it will drive away most of the birds. Blue jays are about the only birds in our yard which will put up a fight and sometimes drive away the squirrel.

The final aspect of feeding birds in winter is concerned with planting certain seed-bearing plants, if space permits. Some birds will feed more readily in the garden if a few plants other than vines, shrubs, tree and the usual garden flowers, are grown. Sunflowers are an example. Many birds will eat sunflower seeds at feeders. But some birds will be attracted more easily if the sunflower heads are left on the stalks where they may be found in a natural way. Goldfinches are an example of birds that come more readily to natural food grown for them.

In some places, game birds such as pheasants, quail and

grouse will come to feed on corn left on the cob, and placed in stalk shelters. Many of the common "weeds," such as crab grass, dock, lambsquarter, amaranths, buttercups, chick-weeds, and wild mustards, produce seeds which are eaten by many birds. If space permits, patches of these "weeds" will provide food for birds.

Feeding birds in winter is fun. It is one of the best ways to get to recognize different birds. It is an excellent way to attract birds to the yard which may stay on to nest in bird-houses put out for them, or in natural nesting sites developed for that purpose. But it is fun in itself, if your only purpose is to watch birds in the yard.

Winter foods	*Birds that may be attracted*
Mixed seeds (hemp, millet, kaffir corn, cracked corn, etc.)	Cowbird, grackle, red-wing, fox sparrow, white-throated sparrow, tree sparrow, song sparrow, field sparrow, vesper sparrow, catbird, brown thrasher, hermit thrush, purple finch, house finch, pine siskin, goldfinch.
Sunflower seeds	Evening grosbeak, pine grosbeak, cardinal, goldfinch, chickadee, nuthatches, purple finch, blue jay.
Cut up pieces of fruit, (apples, banana, etc.) wild fruit such as bay-berry, currants	California thrasher, brown thrasher, robin, hermit thrush, catbird, bluebird, downy, hairy and red-headed woodpeckers, flicker, myrtle warbler.

Suet	Downy and hairy woodpeckers, red-breasted and white-breasted nuthatches, chickadee, flicker, tufted titmouse, blue jay, brown creeper, some sparrows, golden-crowned kinglet, red-winged blackbird.
Peanut butter, nutmeats	White-breasted nuthatch, downy woodpecker, chickadee, blue jay, tree sparrows, fox sparrows, tufted titmouse, house finch, purple finch, pine and evening grosbeaks, cardinal, catbird.
Breadcrumbs, doughnuts, cold cereals	Brown thrasher, catbird, blue jay, chickadee, purple finch, sparrows, junco, tufted titmouse, cardinal, downy woodpecker, Carolina wren.

CHAPTER 6

EVERY DAY IS SATURDAY NIGHT

IF YOU enjoy watching birds feed in your yard during the winter, you have even greater pleasures in store, come spring. For in most places, bird baths will replace the feeder as the center of interest, and spring and summer birds, with their brilliant plumage and musical songs, make the winter visitors seem drab indeed. Birds need water as much as food and cover for survival, and frequently fly quite a distance to get it. Dry seasons are especially good times to provide all the water possible, and the birds that come to drink and dunk make any efforts expended well worthwhile.

It was not until we visited the Roosevelt Bird Sanctuary at Oyster Bay, Long Island, that we appreciated the value of water as a means of attracting birds. There, in a very few minutes we saw fifteen different birds at a small artificial, yet natural-looking pool back along the Sanctuary trail. Orioles, scarlet tanagers, catbirds, brown thrashers, wood thrushes, robins, towhees, warblers of several varieties, crested flycatchers, blue jays and a flicker, all come to bathe within

Top—A homemade bird bath using a trash-can top and a section of iron or clay pipe. This bath has the advantage of being able to withstand ice without cracking.

Bottom—A garden pool will attract birds to the garden as well as provide a suitable place to grow interesting plants.

twenty feet of our observation post. The most we ever saw at our "store bought" bath at home was a robin or two and occasionally a song sparrow. We wondered why the birds flocked to that bath, and so thoroughly avoided ours. Water was water, wherever it was, but then we realized the difference.

We remembered watching birds at the natural places where they found water, streams and ponds. First of all, the water there was moving. There were ripples that sparkled in the sunlight. There was the sound of water running down over the rocks or lapping against the rocky or sandy shore. These were the two qualities of water lacking in our bird bath, movement and sound. Then too, the water along the edge of the stream was quite shallow, only an inch or two deep and it got progressively deeper. A bird could walk in, instead of having to dive as in the case of the cup-shaped bath in our garden.

The natural pools at the Roosevelt Sanctuary closely resembled the small pools of a hillside spring. They were shallow excavations in the dirt, lined with cement. The pools were two to three feet in diameter and about two-inches deep in the middle. One pool was above the other, on the slope, and they were connected with a cement drain. Thus, water overflowing the top pool would drain into the lower pool, some twenty feet below. There was no natural water supply, so water had been piped to the upper pool where the slow flow was regulated with an ordinary faucet. The water dripped out just enough to cause ripples, and to overflow the pool to fill the one below.

Around the edges of the pools, rocks had been set in the

cement to provide perches on which birds might sit to shake
and preen. Surrounding the two pools were shrubs and trees
that provided cover and perches.

Taking a lesson from nature, and from the successful
experience at Oyster Bay, we revised our home baths with
considerably better results. Now it is quite common to see
some fifty species of birds use the bath in the course of the
year, and not single individuals of a species either. Several
birds have come with their young, and many a fledgling
robin, blue jay, oriole, catbird, yellowthroat, grackle, tanager
and song sparrow have we watched take its first bath. On
many occasions the hydrangea, Japanese maple, willow and
rambler roses are filled with other birds. waiting their turns.

Our bird baths are not as natural appearing as those at
Oyster Bay. Our side of Long Island is as flat as the proverbial
pancake, and we have no hillsides to use. But a little cement,
some discarded trashcan lids and a few lengths of hose have
provided the means of attracting birds to the garden all year
long, but especially in summer and early fall.

First, we made two cement pools, one in the flowergarden,
and one further from the house, out in the vegetable garden.
These were similar to the pools at the Sanctuary. We made
them by digging out a shallow round hole four inches deep
and three feet in diameter. We smoothed out the bottom.
Then we mixed cement at the ratio of four parts gravel to
one part cement. The ingredients were mixed dry on some
boards nailed together, until we had a uniformly colored
mixture. Then water was added and mixed until the cement
was thin enough to apply, but not thin enough to "run" and
fill in the hole with a solid block of cement.

Top—A trash-can top placed low to the ground will provide a bath for many birds that avoid one that is higher up.

Bottom—For formal garden layouts, a traditional pottery bath is useful and attractive.

The first layer was an inch or so thick. We then cut some strips from an extra piece of window screening and placed them across the hole, molding them into the cement. Then we added another layer of cement an inch or so thick. When the cement dried thoroughly in three or four days, we had a "basin" that was two inches deep in the middle and barely a quarter-inch deep at the edges. In the center we placed a large rock as a perch and place to dry.

To get ripples in the pool we tried two devices, one temporary, the other permanent. First we used an old coffee can and punched a small hole in the bottom. We whittled out a peg and plugged the hole from the inside, enough to allow twenty or thirty drops a minute to leak through. Then we hung the can over the pool. The dripping water sounded like dripping water, strangely enough, and caused ripples to run outward from the center. The experiment worked, so we hooked up the permanent device.

From a nearby faucet, we stretched an old section of hose to a young maple near the pool. To the end of the garden hose we attached a smaller rubber tube, and ran it up the tree, and out on a branch, so the end was about two feet over the pool. Careful regulation of the faucet gave a dripping that answered our purpose. Before long, birds found the pool and came regularly to bathe and drink.

But we wanted to keep a bath filled all winter and we were afraid that water freezing in the cement would crack it, and being allergic to mixing cement to patch the cracks, we built two more baths. Both of these were made of trashcan tops, about eighteen inches in diameter and three or four inches deep. We partly filled the tops with pebbles to cut down the depth to two or two and a half inches, and also to add weight.

One can top was placed on the ground where we keep it filled with water all year round. In the winter we filled it with hot water twice a day. The ice that forms is easy to chip out. The second top we placed in a low fork of an apple tree, about four feet from the ground.

In winter, birds use these baths chiefly for drinking but some of the more hardy species bathe on the coldest days. Tree sparrows, juncos, cowbirds, downy woodpeckers and several others will spend several minutes splashing around before they fly off to the hedge to dry off and rearrange their feathers.

Another type of winter bird bath was suggested to us by Dr. Richard Weaver, former director of the Audubon Nature Center, Greenwich, Connecticut. It consisted of a flat, tin pieplate fastened on the open top of an old coffee can. In the coffee can was mounted an electric light socket, with a forty watt bulb screwed in it. A wire ran from the socket to an outlet in the house. The heat from the bulb kept the water in the pan from freezing and thus provided drinking water all day. We built such a bath and placed it on the windowsill. The only problem was that on a busy day it required filling several times a day. The other baths would freeze up, but that one remained reasonably warm. Sparrows, jays, downies, cowbirds, red-wings and chickadees flocked to it all day long. To the best of our knowledge a bath such as this must be a homemade job. There are none that we know of on the market.

In general there are two other rules for bird baths for the greatest success in attracting birds. Most important, probably, is that there must be good cover close by through which birds may approach the bath, and to which they may go after bathing. It frequently happens that when birds bathe, their feathers become so soaked that they are unable to fly, or can only fly a short way until they dry off. They can fall easy prey to cats or hawks in this condition, and need suitable cover for protection. Some birds like to look the situation over before bathing, and need a suitable perch as a look-out.

Bird baths usually should be placed in shade or semi-shade. In direct sun the water will heat up in summer, and apparently, birds prefer water as cool as possible. Our baths in the shade have always been more popular than those in sunlight. We have planted tall-growing, rather dense annuals or shrubs on the south side of the baths that cannot be moved. This provided the necessary shade, and kept the water cool enough so that soon birds were attracted to them.

Other types of baths that have proved successful are rustic in appearance. We saw one bath that was most attractive looking and attractive to birds. It consisted of a pile of stones picked up nearby and arranged in a natural-looking pile about three feet high, four feet in diameter at the bottom and two feet in diameter on top. The top of the bath was a shallow pool made of cement. The rocks were held in place with cement. At the bottom of the rock pile was a semicircular pool, also of cement, about a foot wide, two inches deep, and extending half-way around the rocks. A pipe ran up through the center of the rocks into the top pool. The end of the pipe was flush with the bottom of the pool. The pipe ran into the cellar of the home, where the water flow was controlled with a valve. Near the pool was another valve for regulating the flow into the pool. At first, water was turned on full until the top pool was full, and overflowed to the crescent-shaped lower pool. Then the flow was cut down to a mere trickle, just enough to keep the lower pool full and overflowing a little. Wild plants that required a moist soil were planted around the edges, and their flowers alone were worth the time and energy it took to build the bath. But the cardinals, thrushes, titmice, orioles and tanagers that came there daily were even more colorful than the flowers.

A very simple bath that is easy to make and which will not crack in freezing weather consists of a wooden mixing bowl bolted to a post. Two wood screws will hold it, and the water will soon swell the wood so that it will leak through the holes made by the screws.

As with houses and sometimes with feeders, birds can be perverse creatures when it comes to using baths. In a town where we once lived, the garden club and the local bird club had collaborated to erect a rather large and expensive fountain-bird bath in memory of John James Audubon. The dedication took place some years before our time, but the story lingered on, and was told to us by one of the older residents in town.

The fountain had been built in a very well-planned and well-kept (for birds) park. During the winter several feeders were placed there and kept filled by members of the garden club. Quite a few birds nested in surrounding wooded areas (now replaced by apartment houses). There was every indication that birds would flock to the bath once they knew where it was.

On the morning of the big day it rained. Several poorly-

drained sections of the small park formed large puddles, and
one such puddle was right beside the small speakers platform
built for the occasion. No one thought much about it at the
time, but that afternoon, it was the puddle and not the fountain that was the center of attraction.

A relative of Audubon was the featured speaker, and was
introduced by one of the founders of the then young Audubon Society. The garden club ladies were out in full attend-
ance as was the bird club. The ceremony was purposely
scheduled for late afternoon for that was the time when the
songs of the wood thrush, oriole, tanager, robin and vireos
were most likely to ring out from the woods, and when these
birds seemed likely to visit the bath. The birds cooperated to
the fullest, with one slight exception. They flocked to the
mud puddle instead of the memorial fountain. They waded
and drank, splashed and dunked, for more than an hour, amid
eloquent talks on the beautiful fountain, which by attracting
so many colorful birds would add so much to the aesthetic
life of the community. Not even an English sparrow sipped
a drop from the fountain that afternoon. But many birds
enjoyed the puddle to the fullest.

The largest number of different birds that we ever saw at
one watering place was in a puddle in the middle of country
dirt. It was immediately after a flash summer rain that broke a
dry spell of several weeks. It poured for about an hour, and
soon after the sun came out it was as hot as before. But the
rain had accumulated in the clay soil and a reddish-brown
puddle was one of the most interesting places we ever saw.

In the hour or so that we watched from a nearby stonewall
not more than forty feet away, and wholly in the open as far

as the birds were concerned, a red-headed woodpecker, meadowlarks, bobolinks, flickers, bluebirds, indigo buntings, goldfinches, cedar waxwings, barn and cliff swallows, robins, a ruby-throated hummingbird, catbirds, red-wings, wrens, a veery, a towhee, a chestnut-sided warbler, a blackburnian warbler, a black-throated green warbler, a redstart, and song sparrows all drank or bathed. Fortunately, no cars passed by to disturb them, or splash the water out of the puddle. It was especially interesting that all these birds should use that puddle when not more than a hundred feet away there ran a clear and cool brook, filled with rocks and shallow enough in places to be suitable for any bird. But that is one of the interesting things about birds. There are several rules that apply to them, but the exceptions to the rules are the most interesting to watch.

One of the interesting things to watching a bird bath is the way that birds approach the bath—that is if there is a sufficient variety of shrubbery nearby to afford a choice of different approaches. It may not be true in all situations, but our observations have shown that almost every bird has its own way of coming up to the bath, and even its own way of bathing.

Jays are not the least bit timid, unless they have young with them. They will streak from a tree twenty feet away, and either fly right to the bath, scaring away anything else there, or they light in a tree over the bath and screech once or twice more just to be noisy, or so it seems. Then they fly down to the edge of the bath where they perch for a moment before jumping into the middle. They splash around for several seconds. Then they hop back to the edge and shake off the water. Back to the middle they jump, to splash around again. Finally, they fly to a tree or shrub to dry off and preen. If their young are with them, they may sneak in through the rosebush, the adults first and then the two or three young. And a family of five jays can soon dehydrate the best bath if a steady flow of water is not provided.

Catbirds are probably the most secretive of all the birds that visit our bath. They invariably come in from the back, spending several minutes in the dense shrubs, hopping around quietly, and apparently looking over the bath from every angle before finally flying to the edge. Then they drink first and frequently hop around for a minute or two before stepping into the water. They then take a quick dip and splash, and jump back to the edge to dry off. They fly back to the hedge to wait a while before the next dip.

Robins use the direct approach. They hop about the lawn searching out worms and grubs, and without much warning, suddenly take off and head right for the bath. They stand on the edge for a second, then in they go. They splash around for several seconds, lying almost flat to get the water up over their backs. They walk over to the edge, shake off the water, then fly off to a favorite perch to rearrange their feathers and preen.

Warblers seem to drop down from above. Directly over one of our baths is a young Japanese maple. The warblers fly to that tree from the nearby apple trees where they feed. The maple is not more than twenty feet high, but warblers come down from the top in ten or twelve stages—scarcely a foot to each stop. At each stop they sit for a moment and look around. Then down to a lower branch. Stop. Look around. Down to another branch. It sometimes takes ten minutes from the time they light in the top of the tree until they finally get their feet wet.

The hummingbirds that visit the garden always seem to drink on the wing. We have yet to see one perch and bathe. From the flowers where they feed, they fly over the bath and hover two or three feet above it for a few seconds. Then drop down, still hovering, sip some water, rise up in the air, wait a second, then drop down for a second sip. They barely dip their needle-like bills in the water before they rise up to hover on their almost invisible wings.

Interesting to watch at the bath are the flycatchers that stop in the garden during migration. We are not sure whether they drink on the wing or whether they are catching insects that are hovering near the water. But they perch in a tree, suddenly dive down over the bath, and then return to the perch. Sometimes they seem to skim the water and sometimes they seem to just miss it. But they return several times before flying off, so perhaps they do exactly what they seem to be doing, drinking sometimes and catching insects at other times.

One day while watching the bird bath, we noticed something rather interesting. We checked on several succeeding days, and the same thing seemed to hold true with very few exceptions. It was the order in which birds used the bath.

Blue jays seemed always to come first in the "social order." If they were in the water, all other birds avoided it, or waited until the jays left. If other birds were in the bath, the jays would drive them away. Next in order came the grackles. They would yield to the jays, but drive other birds away.

Occasionally, starlings might put up a fight, but usually they gave in to jays and grackles and awaited their turn.

Robins came next, giving in to the birds above them but driving others away, followed by thrashers, orioles, catbirds, sparrows and finally warblers, in that order. The English sparrow was the one exception that we noticed. Sometimes that pugnacious bird would fight robins or thrashers, and win out. Sometimes the larger birds would drive them away. Sometimes, too, two birds of different species would use the bath at the same time, or at least one would perch on the edge while the other splashed around. But generally, there was a definite order in which birds used the bath.

Bird baths are interesting not only for the enjoyment gained from watching birds splash around and drink, but for the close-up view that is possible of birds at all times of year. More than once we have thought that we had new birds in the yard as we noticed a bird that we did not recognize. But closer observation usually showed a warbler in fall plumage— the same species that we had seen but two months before in entirely different plumage. Fall warblers are probably the most confusing of all birds to get to know. Their totally different appearance from their bright spring coloring makes them difficult for the experienced birder, much less the beginner. When they flit around tree tops feeding during the day, in preparation for their nightly flights toward the south, identification is difficult. But when they stop at bird baths, and perch in a neighboring tree to dry off, they present a brief close-up that usually is sufficient. Many warblers will not visit the garden, but some do, and frequently many of those that are missed in the spring flight.

Watching birds such as orioles, tanagers, warblers, and even robins, bring their young to the yard for a drink and a bath, also provides an unusual opportunity to compare juvenile with adult plumages. One can scarcely imagine that the drab-looking young orioles will become the beautiful orange and black orioles that will return next spring; or that the mottled young tanagers could become the brilliant scarlet and black-winged birds that will sing from the tree tops eight or nine months later.

Many birds will be attracted to water in the garden. But many too will be attracted to soft, dry dirt. In spring, summer and fall, dirt is rather easy to find for dust baths, and also to provide the grit that is necessary for birds' digestive processes. But in winter, with snow on the ground, dust and grit may not be so easy to find.

Garden seed flats or any flat box make excellent devices to hold ordinary earth or gravel. We usually keep it covered so that rain or snow will not soak it, later to freeze solid. We place two or three of these flats out where birds can find them, and to make sure, we sprinkle some feed on top of the dirt. It is surprising how many birds will use these flats to dust themselves, or for the grit needed to help grind up the hard seeds that they eat.

CHAPTER 7

BIRD PHOTOGRAPHY

ANYONE who has never tried bird photography has some real excitement awaiting. A combination of an interest in birds and skill with a camera can result in thrills that even surpass those found in a duck blind, along a deer run, or on the most primitive trout stream or bass lake. We have tried them all—hunting, fishing and photography, and we still get a bigger kick out of a good bird picture than from netting a three-pound trout or knocking down a canvasback as it wheels over the decoys. And we get good pictures about as regularly as we get three-pound trout—which isn't often. Of course, we are rather critical of bird photographs, and require a sharp definition of a good pose in good composition, with pleasing lighting and a natural background.

Birds are not always the most cooperative models, and frequently play hard to get. When they do flock within camera range, they show a remarkable propensity for facing away from the camera. The resulting photograph of the southern exposure of a northbound bird leaves much to be desired.

We believe that we have the largest collection of such photos in existence, not through choice however. But bird photography is fun, and with a moderate amount of patience and reasonable skill with a camera, anyone can get satisfactory negatives of wild birds.

Whatever your interest in birds, you can add to that interest with bird pictures. If you desire a pictorial record of the birds that visit your feeder, bird bath or birdhouse, or which nest in the yard, you can get such a record rather easily. If your interest lies on the more artistic side, and you want good photographs with birds as the center of interest, you can work a little harder and get them. If your interest lies in the direction of recording interesting habits of the birds that visit your yard, you may have a more difficult job, but it is still great sport in every sense of the word.

Most back yards can be turned into a photography studio for birds with very little trouble. Frequently the job requires no more work than moving feeders, houses or bird baths so as to get better light and better backgrounds. If the birdhouses or feeders look too "man-made" and you desire a more natural setting, a few hours in the basement workshop with rustic materials will do the trick. And bird photography rarely stops in the back yard. Once you get the knack of it, just as in hunting or fishing, there is an ever increasing desire to seek wilder places with a wider variety of birds.

Bird photography has many advantages over hunting. Granted, you cannot eat a negative, or impress the neighbors by coming home with a full bag. But, on the other hand, you need not worry about closed seasons or hunting licenses. You can always ask the neighbors in for a showing of your Kodachromes or mounted prints. The ladies at the garden club will coo and rave over the same pictures or slides at a monthly meeting, and many a school will welcome a showing with many subsequent invitations to come again.

Once you knock down a duck with a load of lead and your dog retrieves the bird, most of the thrill is gone. But the suspense in the darkroom, or waiting at the photo lab counter, is probably greater than the thrill of seeing the cardinal or oriole get in just the right position on the edge of the pool, and stay there long enough for you to trip the shutter and record its permanent image on the sensitive emulsion. We have spent many a hot hour in a blind waiting for birds to hop into focus on feeder or pool, but we know that we have perspired more in the darkroom as the milky emulsion cleared and the image of the bird appeared. Would it be sharp and contrasty? Or had we wasted another hour only to get a fuzzy, flat picture? You can always hope, as you shoot the picture and take the undeveloped results back home. But all hope is gone, or your spirits rise higher than ever, in the darkroom in a very few seconds.

As is the case with most phases of photography, the better equipment will give the more satisfactory results. We know that like all general statements, that one is open to question. We have seen bird pictures taken forty and fifty years ago that we wish we could duplicate with our superior equipment. But we have also seen many more pictures taken by such experts as Allan D. Cruickshank and Roger Tory Peterson in recent years that are masterpieces of photographic art. Their equipment is probably the finest available for this purpose.

Few of us can hope to achieve the success of those outstanding bird photographers. But most of us can get pictures that satisfy us and have fun doing it. We can use almost any camera that we already have, making a few adaptations necessary for this special purpose.

The ideal camera in our opinion for bird photography (and there are many who will raise issue with us) is a 4 x 5 Graflex with double extension bellows. A telephoto lens will help tremendously, but for many pictures it is not absolutely necessary. Of course, for color work, this size is expensive to use, especially considering the high number of misses in bird photography. But for black and white, when enlargements are desired, this large size negative is hard to beat.

Next in preference comes the smaller size reflex and graphic type cameras, either with double extension bellows, or extension tubes, permitting the use of longer focal length lenses and ground glass focusing.

Finally in preference for black and white, but perhaps first for color, come the 35 millimeter cameras. But again, telephoto lenses, or extension tubes and supplementary lenses, are required for best results.

Our reasons are based on our own experience. The average song bird taken at eight feet will register so small on a 2¼ x 3¼ negative, using a standard lens, that a tremendous enlargement is necessary to get a reasonably sized print. The camera cannot be used much closer to the bird, since the bird will be frightened and will not come within range.

We have had birds perch right on the camera, but only after becoming used to it for several hours. During migration, when the largest numbers of birds visit the bath or feeder, you do not have time to let them get used to seeing that queer black box so close to the food they want.

Consequently, some system of magnification is necessary— either a telephoto lens, or a supplementary lens attached over the standard lens. Both of these devices require double extension bellows or an extension tube (or moving back further from the bird which leaves you where you were before you put on the longer focus lens).

Ground glass focusing is the best, in our opinion, for the critical focusing necessary to get really sharp images. Rangefinders work very well, it is true, but working at eight feet, frequently with the lens at its widest aperture, makes ground glass the surer means of getting good pictures. Sometimes too, you want to work at distances too close for rangefinders.

Not for a minute do we want to discourage anyone whose equipment does not conform to these standards. We are describing what we consider best for bird photography. Many an inexpensive folding or box camera will give remarkable results if a portrait attachment may be used, and if the photographer is careful as well as skillful with what equipment he uses.

As far as shutter speeds are concerned our experience in back yard photography has shown that one one-hundredth of a second is average with a compur shutter, and a two-hundredth with a focal plane shutter. The reason is that the compur opens and closes with a quick click, and by the time the birds jump, their picture is taken. But the unwinding of the focal plane shutter causes a sound that startles them, and they jump just about as the picture is taken. Blurred images result with slower speeds with a focal plane shutter. The shutters on the less expensive cameras are in the class with the compur. There is no noise to startle the bird until the picture is actually taken.

Again, cameras with slower speeds may be used quite successfully but more care is necessary.

Three other pieces of equipment are highly desirable for successful bird photographs: a tripod, a flash gun of some sort, and a remote control device.

Almost any sort of tripod is satisfactory, as long as it is sturdy enough to support the camera, and as long as it is easily adjustable. It should be possible to adjust the height quickly and easily, and to tilt the camera to any angle.

An attachment that synchronizes the flash of the bulb with the opening of the shutter at speeds from one fiftieth to one two-hundredth is ideal. Many new cameras have built-in synchronization which is better yet. Then, all that is required is a battery case and reflector for the bulb.

It may seem strange that with bird pictures being taken outdoors, that flash bulbs are suggested, but there are two good reasons for it. Frequently bird pictures must be taken in shade, where slow shutter speeds and wide lens apertures would be required were it not for the artificial light. With flash bulbs, the densest shrubbery can still yield some excellent shots of nesting birds. For color work, and even with black and white, flash is handy to fill in shadows and to get detail that is impossible with natural light conditions.

One of the chief uses of flash bulbs, though, is based on the fact that most bird photography is done on days when clouds may pass over the sun (which is most days in spring or fall). It is easy to set the lens and shutter for full sunlight on a bird, then sit back and wait for the bird to come. But in the few intervening minutes, a billowy white cloud blows over, and the light drops off considerably. Just then the bird hops into range. If you take the picture, it may be under-exposed completely, or enough so to ruin it. But with a flash bulb synchronized with the shutter, and set at a 45 degree angle to the camera, clouds may come and go and you may still get perfectly exposed pictures.

There is one more very useful purpose for flash bulbs. Frequently, the tone in black and white of the bird closely resembles that of the background. With natural light, the bird may blend into the shrubbery so as hardly to be visible. But a flash bulb will light up the bird and background in varying degrees of exposure which sets the bird out from the background on the negative. The bird, being closer to the bulb, will be perfectly exposed. But the background will be a little underexposed due to the fading light further from the source.

The remote control device may be combined with the flash gun. With our gear it is. On the back of the battery case is a device where a wire may be connected, which, when contact is made, will fire the bulb and release the shutter simultaneously from several feet away.

Thus it is possible to set the camera on a tripod near the bird bath, and focus it on the bath. We then run the wire into the house, fifty feet away, and sit inside the window awaiting the arrival of our camera subjects. A doorbell button on the end of the lamp cord is our release switch. When the bird lights in the desired position, we push the button and take the picture.

Without that type of rig, an improvised remote control device may be made. One of the best we know is made from a hinge, rubber bands, a metal cable release, a stick of wood and a long piece of string. The illustration on page 172 shows how to use this device.

Birds are easily photographed at feeder or bird bath using a simple remote-control device.

Fasten the hinge on the tripod so that it opens and closes easily. Place the cable release through a screw hole in the hinge so that the closing hinge will press the release and open the shutter. Then, fasten two or three strong rubber bands around the hinge so as to hold it closed. Force it open with a small stick of wood, or a small nail, to which a piece of nylon fish line or other strong cord is attached. When you pull the string and yank out the stick, the hinge closes and releases the shutter. Rube Goldberg could not do better. But be sure to try out the device, holding the tripod firmly with one hand. If the stick of wood does not pull out easily it is possible to pull over the entire tripod and possibly damage the camera.

The choice of black and white film will depend largely upon the size of the negative and whether or not you use flash to get more light in dark places. Since enlargements must be made, the finer grain of film you can use, the better. With many pictures grain does not detract too much. But with birds, it seems to us, too much grain in the print is objectionable. Of course, fine-grain developers may be used with coarse-grained films, but generally these developers are less contrasty and tend to "flatten" the picture. That has been our experience, anyway.

For negatives of 2¼ x 3¼ or larger, we prefer a moderate speed panchromatic film with a Weston rating of about fifty. These films have good contrast and will take moderate enlargement, even with fast, contrasty developers. In most cases we use flash bulbs, so as to get added light.

For negatives smaller than 2¼ x 3¼ and especially with the 35 millimeter size, we suggest a fine-grain film. Otherwise, when you blow up a negative 10 diameters, grain is bound to show up to some extent. Unfortunately, most of the fine-grain films are rather slow and in many cases flash will be necessary.

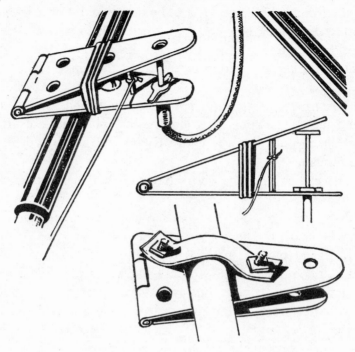

Details of a remote-control gadget for bird photography. Thread a cable release through hole in a small hinge. Attach hinge to a tripod leg. Fasten rubber bands around the hinge to hold it closed, which presses the release and opens shutter. Prop the hinge open with a nail to which a long string is attached. Pull the string to take the picture.

There are many times, naturally, when the "super" films are used. When you can get the camera close to a nest or feeding spot, and when you know that extreme enlargements will not be necessary, such films are ideal. The speed makes it possible to close down the aperture and get greater depth of focus, and consequently, greater detail in the bird.

A general rule that we always follow is to use the smallest aperture possible and the slowest shutter speed that will stop action. (Another reason for flash boosters.) When the camera is only eight feet or so from the bird, and a long focal-length lens is used, the depth of focus is very short. You need every sixteenth of an inch you can get. Consequently, the smallest aperture it is possible to use, is best to get this added depth. Many a picture may be ruined by having a bird half in focus and half out. Many shots are of birds facing an angle into the camera. The bird may be only six inches long, but this may be greater than the depth of focus with the lens wide open at eight feet. If you focus on the head, the tail is fuzzy. If you focus on the middle, both ends are just fuzzy enough to lose the feather detail you want. Hence, the rule of getting all the depth of focus possible, with the smallest lens aperture possible.

The same general rules apply to color film. Our experience has been that flash is almost always necessary with Koda-chrome. We have used outdoor film and blue bulbs, exposing by the formula for flash, and disregarding the natural light. Color film is so much slower than black and white that arti-ficial light is almost a necessity, except in rare cases.

One suggestion for using flash is to try to avoid having the bulb right at the camera. Rig up an extension wire—three or four feet is all that is necessary—and place the bulb at a 45 degree angle to the camera and bird. The resulting modeling on the bird will show the reason for this. When using sun-light alone as the main source of light, forget that rule about having the sun come over your shoulder. (Except with color) try to set up the camera so that the sun is at a 45 degree angle to the camera and bird. You get much better detail in the feathers with that sort of lighting.

Reflectors come in handy too, to fill in shadows and to give a little backlighting. Reflectors about 18 inches by 24 inches are easy to make. When placed just right they will reflect light on the background and on the bird. We use pieces of composition board, such as Celotex or masonite, which have been painted white, or to which sheets of aluminum foil have been stapled or tacked. Since aluminum foil has become readily available in most places, we prefer to use it. It has greater reflecting power and is easy to keep clean and shiny. A forty-foot roll costs only a cent a foot, and has many other uses around the home.

Once you get a camera of some sort, and a long focus lens, or supplementary lens to go over the standard lens, the balance of the equipment necessary for bird photography may be improvised. It is not too difficult when you know what you want and get down to the job of making it.

Using the equipment is another matter. Generally, bird pictures in the yard may be taken in two ways—by remote control, or from a blind. Occasionally, a bird will become so tame that you can walk up, focus on it, take a picture, change the film, cock the shutter and take another. We had such an experience with a Carolina wren.

It was a beautiful September day, and we were on a jetty extending out into the ocean, taking pictures of sandpipers. We were lying flat on a rock, focusing on some sandpipers about ten feet away. Something touched our shoe, and we looked around to see a wren perching on our heel. We turned over and sat up, being rather careful not to frighten the bird. But the wren was too close for our rangefinder and 12 inch lens. We backed up a few feet, but the bird calmly hopped after us, always too close for a picture. This went on for five minutes, with the tame wren sometimes being only three feet or less from the lens.

Finally we reached into our pack, and took out our standard 4 inch lens and replaced the telephoto. It was then easy to take half a dozen pictures of the wren in as many poses. Finally, we went back to photographing the sandpipers with the long lens, and the wren followed us for half an hour, never getting more than ten feet away.

Another time, it was a saw whet owl that reversed the usual procedure and was an ideal model. We found the bird in a spruce tree just outside a window. We watched it for several minutes, then got the camera. We opened the window, and the bird scarcely blinked an eye. It was too dark there for critical focusing with either ground glass or rangefinder, so we resorted to the primitive ruler, and measured exactly three feet from the bird to the camera. We set the camera for three feet, rigged up the flash attachment at two feet and at 45 degrees from the camera, and took our first picture.

The owl blinked. In fact he closed one eye and opened the other. But we did not move an inch. We took half a dozen pictures in ten minutes of the best model, human or otherwise, that we ever had.

But those were exceptions. Normally, you spend much more time, and need much more elaborate arrangements to get satisfactory pictures.

Most pictures in the yard probably will be taken by remote control—that is, setting up the camera and focusing it on a fixed spot—then moving back several feet to wait the bird's arrival. This is where the feeders, bird baths or bird boxes come in handy.

Suppose that it is winter. Sparrows, juncos, blue jays, cardinals, or grosbeaks are visiting the feeder you stock with seeds. You want to get portraits of them—close-up shots that would be nice to frame and hang in the study. Here is one way to do it.

Watch the birds at the feeder for half an hour or so. You will see that they generally follow the same procedure as they come to feed. They will perch in a bush or tree. Then they will fly down and light in one place on the feeder, probably the highest point. They will then drop down to the feed itself and start to peck at the seeds.

When you know what their habits are, and just about what they will do, set up the camera on the tripod, focused on the point where they light first, or on the point where they start to feed. This point should be as small as possible. Let us say that the feeder has a roof with a ridge; or it is a window feeder with a strip of wood along the front edge. The birds will usually perch first on the ridge or on that strip of wood. Set up the camera so the ridge or strip is parallel with the plane of the film. Thus, any point on that ridge or strip of wood will be in focus. Other points on the two feeders will probably be out of focus.

When the camera is set up, focused, the shutter cocked, the remote control device in working order and film in place, run the remote control string or cable to a place where you can wait in comfort. Our pet spot is just inside the dining-room window, fron which warm place we can see the feeder very easily.

Then the wait begins. At first the birds are wary of the camera. They flutter by but will not stop to feed. In a few minutes though, they usually get used to it and resume their normal activities.

Sometimes it may be necessary to resort to a trick or two to save time in getting birds accustomed to the camera. One way is to camouflage it with boughs, sticks, grass or straw so that it closely resembles the natural background. Try to make the camera on the tripod look like a tree or shrub. But do not drape a piece of cloth over it or a burlap bag. We tried that once, and birds would not approach the feeder at all. Apparently, the camera looked like a man standing there and frightened the birds more than the camera alone.

Another stunt is to place the tripod near the feeder several hours in advance of the time when you want to use it. Place a box on top to simulate the camera. The birds will get used to it, and when you replace the box with the camera, they never know the difference.

In taking pictures in this way, place the camera in such a position that when the bird perches on the ridge or rim, it is backed by unbroken shrubbery, or better yet, the sky. Avoid taking the bird against the feeder itself. In black and white the tone values are not varied enough for good contrast. It may be possible to arrange a backdrop far enough behind so that it would be out of focus, but which would provide an even background. We once set up a feeder about ten feet from a blank side of the garage and used the garage wall for a background.

With a little planning, it is possible to get bird pictures at a feeder that do not show the feeder at all, but rather look as if the picture were taken in a perfectly natural spot. The secret is to capitalize on the habit of most birds to perch in a tree or shrub for a second to look the situation over before starting to feed. The system we use is this:

Set two poles in the ground, about eighteen inches apart, one post being three feet high and one being four or five feet high. On the top of the low post fasten a flat tray of some sort—shallow pan, cheese box, or homemade wooden tray, about eight by ten inches and an inch deep. Fill the tray with seeds, ground-up suet, nutmeats or anything that will attract birds.

Then, drill a hole near the top of the longer pole on the side toward the shorter pole. Cut a branch from an evergreen, or other tree or shrub, and stick it in the hole so that it extends out over the food tray. Most birds will perch for a second on the branch before darting down to the tray.

Again, it is important to arrange the camera so that the branch is parallel with the plane of the film. Thus if the bird lands on any part of the branch, it is in focus. Otherwise, you must wait and hope for the bird to perch in just the right place.

Frequently it is possible to use this same device to attract birds such as nuthatches, downies or chickadees. Arrange the branch in a natural position, as if it were growing on a tree. Then pour melted suet over it. The birds will come to feed on the suet, and click—another picture.

Generally, it is best to try for one or two birds at a time, unless you have a special reason for wanting a picture of a flock. It is difficult to get more than one or two in focus at once, and several fuzzy images in the background or foreground detract from the attractiveness of the picture. Another successful stunt for getting woodpeckers, nuthatches or creepers is to place a regular suet-holder low enough on the trunk of a tree so that it is easy to photograph. When the birds are accustomed to using it, take it off the tree and pour some melted suet down the bark in the exact spot where the suet-holder was fastened. You might push some soft suet or nutmeats into the cracks in the bark instead. Then place the camera on one side of the tree so that as the birds feed you get a profile shot. It will be possible to get such a picture without the suet showing up, and the trick of baiting the bird to the tree will not be obvious. Of course, replace the filled suet-holder when you are through so the birds will continue to come to the same place.

While we have taken hundreds of pictures at feeders, our best results have been at a bird bath. The bath was the natural-looking, artificial pool on the ground. On one side of the pool was a rock that stuck up four or five inches higher than the rim of the pool. Observation, for an hour or so, showed that most birds would perch on that rock for a minute or two before bathing. Since the top of the rock was only an inch or so square, it was an ideal focal point, and we knew that any bird which stood there would be in focus. At that spot, in four hours one day, we photographed robins, blue jays, orioles, catbirds, tanagers, towhees, sparrows, warblers, and chickadees—eleven species in all. It was in dense shade and flash was necessary, but the results were well worth it. Coming home to our yard, we applied the same principle, supplying a small perch on the edge of our bath for a stopping place for the birds that visited it. The perch was no more than a rock, set in the bath so that it stuck five or six inches out of the water. By lowering the camera on the tripod to about the level of the bird, we could focus on the perch, and shoot over top of the bath. All the pictures showed were the rock perch with a bird on top against a dark background of shrubbery. The bird was in direct sunlight, but the shrubbery was in shade, and consequently underexposed enough to give good contrast with the chief subject of interest.

For year round photography, the bird bath will prove to be the most satisfactory place to operate. Birds need water in winter and summer, spring and fall, and more different birds, probably, will visit the bath than any other one spot in the yard. Consequently, it is well worth while to build a natural looking bath, surrounded by plants that photograph well— generally those with large leaves. It pays to build "perches" over or beside the bath which birds will come to use regularly. Then you can get birds in natural poses on branches and twigs as well as on the perch in the bath.

Photographing birds at a birdhouse is much the same as picture-taking at the feeder. Generally, the houses are in the open where you can watch them from a distance and trip the camera shutter by remote control. Usually you will have more difficulty getting successful pictures at the birdhouse than at the feeder or bird bath. Birds will not generally perch on the house or linger long at the entrance. They fly up to the house quickly, sit for a second at the entrance, then dive inside. While perching at the entrance, they are usually looking inside, so the only view the photographer gets is the back without the head.

The last time we tried to get photos of bluebirds at the nest we used twelve negatives to get two satisfactory pictures. We had set the camera at one of the apple trees in which the nest was located and tried to get profile pictures as the female came to feed her young. But the actions were too fast for us and the largest percentage of the pictures were of a bluebird's tail sticking out the hole in the tree. We watched carefully so as to get the bird the instant it poked its head out of the hole, just before flying away for more food. But usually we were too slow. Anyway, we got good pictures of the hole in the apple tree.

We even tried the old squeaking trick to try to attract the bird's attention as it alighted at the entrance with a mouthful of insects. It generally works, but not with those bluebirds. It is a good trick to know because it will usually make birds perk up and look around. Just kiss the back of your hand loudly, so you make a sort of squeaking noise. Apparently the noise sounds like young birds in distress for it certainly attracts the attention of the adult birds. The trick works best in spring and summer, but it will also be effective in many cases at other times of the year.

There is some danger in photographing birds at bird boxes or nests. The camera, or you, may frighten the adult birds so that they stay away so long the eggs get chilled and the embryos die. Or they may neglect to feed the young for a while. They may even desert the nest entirely if you remain nearby for too long a time. A few pictures are hardly worth that, so be careful If you photograph birds at a nest in the yard, be especially careful about not moving branches or twigs that get in the way. You may let in sunlight that will be too strong for the young birds, or frighten the adults away. You may show a lurking cat the location of the nest, and that is the end of the young.

But with a little care it is possible to get excellent pictures of birds on the nest. Song sparrows, catbirds, robins, thrashers, wood thrushes, some warblers, cuckoos, cardinals, mockingbirds, grackles, jays, and other birds, all will nest around the yard in some places and make very interesting pictures, especially in color. It is possible, rather easily, to get a whole series of pictures at one nest: Building the nest, the first egg, the next eggs, incubating the eggs, the newly-hatched young, feeding the young, the young as they grow up, and finally, the young as they walk out on a branch and stretch their wings preparing for their first flight. Of all the bird pictures that have been taken, it is surprising how few such series of pictures there are. Most photographers are satisfied with one or two pictures and overlook the marvelous opportunity to get a picture-story of wild birds at home.

Remote control is not always the best method of getting such pictures. Many times a blind will be necessary. A blind is some kind of shelter in which you hide, built near the nest. The camera is set up inside and the lens protrudes through a slit in the side.

One of the easiest kinds of blind to make is with a large beach or lawn umbrella as a base. Drive the pole into the ground so that the umbrella stands solidly in place. Then with safety pins fasten some opened-up burlap bags, or strips of muslin, to the top of the umbrella so that you have a tent.

Stake down the burlap or muslin sides so they do not flap in the breeze. Nothing will frighten the birds quite so fast.

Cut a slit in one side, near the nest, and set up and focus the camera. Surprisingly enough, birds will accept this new piece of landscape rather quickly and go about their business in a normal fashion. It will not be long before they are not even frightened by the click of the shutter.

Sometimes it helps to cover the blind with boughs or branches to give it a more natural look. But usually burlap or other drab-colored material blends into the background and will not frighten away your camera subjects.

Any small tent will do for a blind if the nest is near the ground. But since many hours may be spent there, if you get the kick out of bird photography that we do, try to devise a blind that is comfortable. It should have ample head room, and should be made of coarse-woven material so that it does not get too hot inside.

The chief advantage of the blind over remote control is that you are much closer to the bird and can pay more attention to composition. When you are only a few feet away you can wait for exactly the pose you want and not gamble as much as you would with taking pictures from a distance. With a reflex camera you can watch the bird on the ground glass all the time and release the shutter at the most desirable moment. On top of that, there is less chance of frightening the bird than there is when you walk up to the camera to change the film and cock the shutter for another exposure by remote control.

You may find that a blind near the bird bath is preferable to a remote control device. It certainly is possible to take more pictures in a short length of time from a blind than by the other method.

But there are pictures that must be taken by remote control, unless you like the idea of building a blind twenty feet up in a tree, and sitting there for an hour or more. We will take remote control.

Robins in our yard prefer the higher forks of the fruit trees, or the higher branches of the spruce. Our method of photographing them was to get one of those gadgets, made by the Eastman-Kodak Company, that has a tripod screw with a ball-bearing socket at one end, and a strong clamp on the other. Thus, it is possible to clamp the gadget on the limb of a tree, fasten the camera to it, attach the remote control wire, and climb down to a more comfortable place to watch and wait. When there are no convenient branches nearby, we lash a pole between two branches, or to one branch, fasten the gadget to the pole, and thus get the camera nearer to the nest.

Of course, it would be easier sometimes to scour the neighborhood and find a more convenient robin nest. But we like to photograph the birds that nest in the yard.

Bird photography is a fascinating hobby in itself, but the by-products are equally interesting. Few people, aside from professional or extremely serious amateur ornithologists, have the patience to sit in one place and watch birds for any length of time. But with the stimulus of watching them in order to get good pictures, you see many interesting things that you might otherwise miss. You must watch birds for long periods of time to genuinely appreciate the lives they live, to understand their habits, and the reason they do some of the things they do. Many phases of bird behavior are not yet understood by ornithologists. Perhaps some of your observations, as you watch them at the nest, at feeders, or at bird baths, may add to scientific knowledge.

As you watch birds to photograph them, watch also for interesting or unusual habits. Make notes on what you see and keep records of your observations. These records, in addition to the pictures, will make interesting stories. You will be surprised at how interesting they are a year or two later.

CHAPTER 8

SEE WHAT YOU LOOK AT

Oɴᴄᴇ you are successful in attracting birds to your yard or garden, and get to know them well enough to call them by name, you are ready for one of the big thrills of bird watching—studying habits and individual characteristics, and trying to interpret what you see birds doing. This is really advanced bird watching and takes considerable experience and background. But it is remarkable what amateurs can do in their own yards, or in neighboring parks or woods, that can contribute to the scientific knowledge of birds.

Unfortunately, too many bird watchers confine their activities to identification of birds. They make careful lists of the birds they see during the year. They become experts in identification. Of course, it is fun and an important part of birding. But once you get to know birds reasonably well, it is much more fun to concentrate on one or two species, and watch them very closely for a year or two, so you know their life histories from personal observation. You can read about birds' activities and bird habits, but it is much more fun, and a fascinating hobby, to see some of these things for yourself.

One example of interesting bird behavior that is easy for the average beginner to see is "bird territories." You may have already noticed it, without knowing. Have you ever seen a robin chase another robin from your yard? Or has a usually unobtrusive song sparrow suddenly become a pugnacious little creature that drives all other song sparrows from the neighborhood?

Have you read newspaper accounts, by writers who get a little too cute, about robins flying at windows, auto windshields, auto hub caps or other shiny objects, either on the street or in the yard? It happens almost every year, but the newswriters completely misinterpret birds' actions in an effort to be amusing or generally because of pure ignorance. It is another case of truth being much more interesting than fiction, but in the rush to get the story in the first edition, truth falls by the wayside and fancy and imagination take over.

The first time we saw it happen was many years ago. We did not know the reason for it, but it happened several times and we decided to find out why. We had been sitting in the yard on a mild May day, and the car was parked in the drive about fifty feet away. Suddenly, we heard a series of bird calls that we recognized as coming from a robin, but which were far different from the usual cheery song. We looked around and there was the robin dashing himself at the shiny hub cap as if to bash his brains out. We watched for a minute or two, and then walked over and pried off the cap and placed it in the car. The robin looked at the wheel, then flew off to a tree nearby. We put the hub cap back in place, and twenty minutes later watched the same procedure all over again. This time we moved the car, and then the robin was again at peace with the world.

We were bewildered enough to try to find out the reason for these actions. That was in the days which birders call "Before Peterson," when Dr. Frank Chapman's *Handbook of Birds of Eastern North America* was the bird hobbyists' bible. Fortunately for us, Dr. Chapman was Curator of Birds in New York's American Museum of Natural History, and was always willing to answer questions on birds.

He told us that some birds, among them robins, staked out "territories" in which they nested. The "territories," or birds' back yards, were of varying sizes and shapes, but each bird knew his own boundary almost down to the last blade of grass. If other robins encroached on his territory, even to feed, he would fight them off and drive them away. In turn, he will be driven from other territories if he tries to enter them. In fact, both birds will defend their territory against others of the same species.

When the robin noticed his own image in the shiny hub cap, he thought it was another male. Hence the attempt to drive it away. It was instinct that prompted the robin to fly at the car, and no other reason.

The song sparrow, another common nesting bird in the yard or garden, also stakes out a definite territory and will do its best to drive away intruders. But song sparrows will rarely try to drive away robins, or vice versa. Birds seem to recognize others of the same species and fight them. Some birds, however, will attempt to drive away all other birds, regardless of species. But there are few of these in the list of back yard nesters.

A very interesting experiment may be carried out to determine as closely as possible the exact boundaries and size of a robin's territory. We have tried it for several years with interesting results. First, of course, we must find a robin nest. In our yard, they have nested in one of three places; in a blue spruce, in a Norway maple, or in a pear tree. The trees are all within fifty feet of each other, and all close to the house. Since in five years, robins nested in all three trees, we attempted to find the reason for it. Our conclusions are these: Robins arrive in our area about the first week in April. At first they just feed in the yard, and there may be several birds present. But by the end of April or the first of May, there will be only two birds there, apparently a pair. They mate about that time and build their nest.

If the season has been such that the maple or pear is in leaf at that time, they nest in one of those trees. They demand the shelter provided by the leaves. Those trees have forks ten to twenty feet from the ground which will easily support the nest. But if the season is such that the maple or pear is slow to come into full leaf, then the robins nest in the spruce which provides the necessary cover at any time. Once a storm blew the nest and eggs from the spruce, and the robins nested again. But the second attempt was in the maple, which by then had a thick canopy of leaves.

When the time comes in the spring for birds to breed and lay their eggs, they have to do it. True, they follow a general courtship pattern, and pre-nesting pattern, but they are controlled by instinct. Apparently they have preferences as to nesting sites, but if such a spot is not suitable, they seek a substitute.

The first time we attempted to determine the size and

boundary of the robin territory, the birds nested in the maple in back of the house. The maple is the largest tree on about an acre of land made up of adjoining back yards. Except for three garages, there are no other buildings in this open area. There are several other trees, but most of the land is used as flower or vegetable gardens. Consequently, the robin had about an acre of cleared land, surrounded by houses.

When we first noticed the birds building the nest (both birds were picking up bits of grass, string and paper, and flying into the maple), we placed a small mirror upright on the ground. The mirror was fastened on a wide board, which acted as a base, and also as a "skid." We tied a string to the board so that from fifty feet away, we could pull the mirror along the ground. The mirror was about ten inches wide and twelve inches high, and glass went right down to the ground.

It took the robins a day to discover the mirror and fly at their own images. One bird, the male, would fight the mirror and the other would perch near the nest and call the typical alarm notes.

Then we pulled the mirror away from the nest, a few feet at a time. About ninety feet from the nest, the male lost all interest in the mirror and went back to nest building. A day or so later, we tried the same stunt in the other direction. At two-day intervals we got the east and west boundaries. We found that on two sides the house and the garage formed the limit of the territory, and on the other two sides an arbitrary line across the lawn and down the middle of the garden formed the boundary. These robins had a territory of about three-quarters of an acre, including half apple orchard, and half vegetable and flowergarden. One side was about twice the length of the other, the territory being roughly shaped like a pyramid, with the top flattened off.

Within the territory were two bird baths, and this apparently was the only water available at all times for some distance around. If it did not rain for several days, other robins from neighboring territories would attempt to come to the baths. Sometimes they were successful. At other times, they were driven off. Similarly, on a neighboring playfield, covered with a thick layer of sod but including no trees, seemed to be neutral territory at times, and disputed ground at others. We watched our robins get worms and grubs in the grass, with other robins feeding a hundred feet away. They would fly back to their nests, going in opposite directions. But occasionally, they would fight it out for possession of the area, and our robins usually were driven off.

In other years, the experiment showed similar results, with different shaped territories, but generally, territories of about the same size. Interestingly enough, the house and garage generally formed one side.

It was our experiment on bird territories that made us decide to build several bird baths and place them as far apart as possible around the yard. We wanted to provide water (and places for photography) for as many birds as possible during the summer; and knowing that if a bath was in one territory, other birds would be driven away, we planned to cover as much ground as possible.

Closely associated with breeding and territory is the function of bird song. It is believed that when such birds as robins or song sparrows sing their well-known songs, it is to proclaim the fact that they have "staked their claim" and to warn off other birds.

One of the stories that we had heard from childhood was that robins were singing for rain. The story went, that when it was dry, worms went deep into the ground where robins could not reach them. Thus, the robin would fly to the top of the highest tree and call for rain, to bring the worms up to the surface where they were easily captured. It is easy to see how such a superstition might originate and be believed. As a child, we thought it a wonderful thing. Usually, in a day or two it did rain. (But it rains rather regularly in April and May anyway.) Some of the old-timers then, and now, predict the weather by such natural phenomena, and place a lot of faith in them. You cannot talk them out of their belief, try as you will. Perhaps we are not romantic enough about the power of birds, but at a very early age our faith in robins was broken.

As we watched robins in the yard and listened to them sing, we believed that they were singing for rain. But one robin persisted in singing, even in the middle of a downpour, and when the spring sky cleared, it continued to sing. That began to shake our faith in robins as weather prognosticators. But it was not till many years later that we began to see the reason for bird song. It had nothing to do with weather, but was an instinctive means of protecting the nesting territory.

Watch the robins, song sparrows or other birds around your house. You can see these things for yourself. But some birds may object rather strenuously if you stick your nose too closely into their private affairs. Blue jays and grackles will treat you as a robin treats a rival male.

The first time a pair of jays nested in back of our garage, we found how they will defend their families, even from humans. We were walking past the shrubbery on the way into the garden, when a sudden whistling of wings near— too near—our left ear made us stop and look. The next dive was straight for our face. We instinctively ducked, but not enough to avoid entirely a peck on the top of the head by the angry jay. Never a sound came from the bird, as it dove and pecked at us. During the rest of the year the jays are particularly noisy as they scream at cats or other intruders on their land. But this jay uttered not a call or scream. It only chattered with its beak—like chattering teeth on a cold day—and tried to drive us away by brute force. Our interest was aroused in spite of the jay's antics, and we investigated more closely. There, on a branch was a nest, and the female was still incubating the eggs. It was not until we had approached to within a foot of the nest that she left it, and then only to help her mate fly at our head to drive us off. We are not sure that we voluntarily decided that we had seen enough. Those jays meant business, and their bills are heavy and strong.

A similar experience with grackles proved to us that birds will defend themselves regardless of the size of the enemy— in this case our camera. We had found a nest in a pine, and had set up the camera for a few pictures by remote control. But the birds would not settle down on the nest. They flew at the camera and seemed to peck especially at the bright lens. After twenty minutes we decided we did not want pictures of the grackle nest anyway, and went home.

Other birds, notably killdeer and grouse, have another

method of defending their young which is remarkable to see. If you get too close to the nest, the adult bird will suddenly seem to be the sickest bird you ever saw. It will lie on the ground and struggle along as if its wing were broken and it was in the throes of dying. The first impression is that something happened to the poor creature, and that it is crawling away to die. Your inclination is to pick it up, and you can approach quite close. But just as you get close enough, it flutters off a few feet, and after it you go. This goes on for several minutes until you are quite a long distance from the nest. Suddenly, the bird miraculously recovers, and flies away leaving you with mixed emotions—first that nature is a wonderful thing when a bird can play a trick as clever as this; and second that you are not very bright to be fooled so easily.

One spring day we were playing golf on a Long Island course that was located on the edge of a marsh and sand dune area. As we followed our ball down a fairway, we noticed two other golfers trying to sneak up on an "injured" killdeer. We could hear them talking and they believed that the bird had been hit by a golf ball and had suffered a broken wing. They were trying to catch it to fix the wing.

But as we watched, they chased the "injured" bird for two hundred feet and could never get closer than six feet to it. That display was the best we ever saw. The bird stayed on the ground and struggled along dragging one wing. Sometimes it would go in a circle, at other times in an irregular course across the fairway, but always away from the nest. It never did fly, but the two golfers tired of chasing it. We waited till they came back for their clubs, and told them what was going on. We should have known better. They laughed, and accused us of exaggerating to say the least. We offered to prove it, and soon found the eggs in a depression in the sand, scarcely two feet from the edge of the fairway.

As we stood looking at the two eggs, we were startled by a loud "kill-dee-dee" as the bird flew in a circle around us. Finally, it lit on the ground and started the broken-wing trick again, about ten feet away. This time it was the other wing. We walked away smiling, to the accompaniment of "I'll be damned. I'll be . . ."

There is no doubt about it, birds are interesting to watch and the more you watch them the more interesting they are. If you want more ideas on things to watch for, read two books listed in the last part of this book. Both are written by experienced and well-known men in the field and are written for beginners in birding as well as the old hand: *Guide to Bird Watching* by Joseph J. Hickey, and *Watching Birds* by James Fisher.

Your bird watching hobby will be much more interesting from the very start if you keep records of what you see; not only lists of different birds seen, but notes on what they are doing. You do not need any elaborate record system. An ordinary blank notebook will do. Probably a loose leaf notebook is best, because you can then arrange it easier.

As a start, keep a list of the different birds that visit the yard. It can be done as a family game, or just as a personal list. For several years we have made it a family project.

We made a wall chart on a large piece of poster-board. Across the chart are horizontal lines about one half-inch apart, and there are vertical columns of varying widths; one

one-half inch wide column, one two-inch wide column and a second half-inch column. The board is wide enough for three sets of these three-column units. Starting on the first of January, we list all the birds we see in or over the yard in a year. In the extreme left column goes the date, in the wide column the name of the bird and the number of that species seen, and in the second narrow column the initials of the one who first saw the bird.

This year the first bird on the list is a screech owl. As we returned from a rather late New Year's Eve party, we heard the owl. There was no doubt as to what it was, so we started off our year's yard list with a good bird. By nightfall on the first, we usually have up to ten more birds—juncos, downies, nuthatches, cowbirds, several sparrows, jays, and others. Our list has run over a hundred for several years. But the interesting thing is the comparison with previous years. Now we know about when to expect the first robins, meadowlarks, orioles, tanagers, and warblers in the spring. We know about when to look for tree swallows or night-hawks moving south in the fall. We know when to watch for fall flights of ducks or geese, and spring flights of cormorants going north.

Other notes we keep in a loose leaf binder, where we have from one to ten or more pages on individual species. The pages are filed alphabetically, with the bird name at the top. As we see interesting things, we jot down the date, and a few words on what we saw. This includes such things as when we see birds collecting nesting materials, when we see the nest, how many eggs are in it, how long it takes the eggs to hatch, how long it takes the young to grow up and leave the nest, what we see birds eat, etc.

Most of the time, only a few words go in each day that we watch birds. At other times if we spend an hour or so at one nest, half a page may be written. But over the years we have a collection of interesting notes that probably would bore anyone else to death. But to us they make interesting reading a year or so later, as we remember back to previous experiences. Also, the comparison of observation today, with observations last year or the year before, show us that birds live according to a pattern, and that the pattern changes very little, if at all.

It does not take much time to jot down these notes or observations, and you may not think at first that they are of much interest. But as time goes on and you get to know more about birds, your observations will be keener, your notes more interesting. Try it anyway, for a while, and see how much fun it is.

We do not know how successful we have been in presenting bird watching as a fascinating hobby—not only for individuals, but for the entire family. Perhaps we assume too much, when we assume that because we like it, others will find it so absorbing. But we do know that thousands of people find recreation and release from the tension of everyday living by spending a few hours each week in watching birds. It is one of the best ways of which we know to relax, and forget business or other problems. It is the kind of relaxation that anyone can enjoy—business man, technician, professional man, teacher or housewife. If you do not believe it, visit a meeting of a local bird club. You will find a cross section of the social and economic strata of your community, from top to bottom and from one side to the other. For most of those people, bird watching is fun. But even if they do not see birds, at least they have had a few hours of healthful recreation outdoors.

Bird watching must have something to attract so many people from so many steps of society. We know it has, and we hope that we present it in its true light. We know that it is one hobby we will ride till we die. Other interests come and go, but birding survives them all, just as birds themselves run in cycles of abundance and scarcity. All we can say is, "Try it." It presents its problems sometimes, but it certainly is fun.

BOOKS ABOUT BIRDS

The following list of birds books has been selected on the basis of those which will be most useful to back yard birders or those who are developing an interest in birds for the first time. The books are also listed in the approximate order of usefulness.

It is felt that everyone will need one of the identification guides in the first group. Knowing birds by their names is an important start in a bird watching hobby. Beyond that, we believe that perhaps both, but at least one, of the books in the second group are necessary for the greatest enjoyment over a period of time. In the beginning it is fun to get to know the names of birds, but after that it is much more fun to know something of how birds live.

BIRD IDENTIFICATION HELPS

Field Guide to the Birds by Roger Tory Peterson. Houghton Mifflin Company, Boston, Mass. 1947.

Peterson's famous *Field Guide* has probably been carried on more bird trips by more people than any other one book, and with good reason. The 1000 illustrations (500 in full color), plus the easy-to-read text make it very easy to use in identifying almost any bird found east of the Great Plains. For each species there is a short description of field marks, voice and range, with notes on how to distinguish it from other birds with which it might be confused.

Field Guide to Western Birds by Roger Tory Peterson. Houghton Mifflin Company, Boston, Mass. 1941.

Similar to *Eastern Guide* by same author, but covering birds in Montana, Wyoming, Colorado, New Mexico, Western Texas, Arizona, Utah, Idaho, Washington, Oregon, Nevada and California. The majority of the illustrations in this volume are dia-grammatic black and white drawings and are excellent for identification purposes. There are five color plates.

Audubon Bird Guide by Richard H. Pough. Doubleday and Company, Inc., Garden City, New York. 1946.

Covering some 275 species of birds found east of the Great Plains, this book has 48 plates in full color, and has the advantage of grouping the color plates in one section for easy reference. It limits itself to land birds (those most likely to be seen in the back yard), and the text for each species covers field marks, habits, voice, nest and range. The foreword is especially interesting for beginners. (We would not attempt to suggest which is best for back yard birding—Peterson or Pough. It is suggested that a reader look at both books and select the one that meets personal preference. We, personally, own and use both books.)

How to Know the Birds by Roger Tory Peterson. Mentor Books, New American Library, New York, N. Y. 1949. 35¢.

This latest addition to the list of identification helps covers more than 200 common species in text, and in black and white line drawings and silhouettes by the author. The birds are the common species found in the east. This is an excellent book for the younger birders, and for oldsters too, who want to start with a less expensive volume. The introduction covering what to look for, and the conclusion on where to look for birds, are both fine for the beginner.

BIRD WATCHING HELPS

Guide to Bird Watching by Joseph J. Hickey. Oxford University Press, New York, N. Y. 1943.

After one has come to know some of the common birds by name, he certainly should own this Guide. Separate chapters explain the problems of migration watching, bird counting, bird distribution, and the general art of watching birds. It is fascinat-ing reading and tremendously helpful for anyone wanting to know more about how birds live. The list of bird clubs in the appendix will be helpful for those seeking kindred souls in their neighborhoods.

Watching Birds by James Fisher. Penguin Books, Inc., New York, N. Y. 35¢. 1946.

This inexpensive little book makes very interesting reading, and is packed with facts about how birds live. Although written for British birders, it is nonetheless useful in America because of the references to North American birds and studies made by North American ornithologists. We heartily recommend this book to everyone interested in birds.

Books on Back Yard Birding

The next group of books and pamphlets all relate to back yard birding in various phases. Different approaches to the same subject and different emphasis on various phases of the subject make it worth while to look at the books and perhaps own many of the inexpensive pamphlets.

Audubon Guide to Attracting Birds by John H. Baker. Doubleday and Company, Inc., Garden City, N. Y. 1941.

Birds in the Garden by Margaret McKenny. Reynal and Hitchcock, Inc., New York, N. Y. 1939.

The ABC of Attracting Birds by Alvin M. Peterson. The Bruce Publishing Company, Milwaukee, Wis. 1937.

Song Bird Sanctuaries by Roger T. Peterson. National Audubon Society, New York, N. Y., 25¢.

An excellent pamphlet setting forth a few general rules for making a natural area more attractive to birds. Many of the rules may be applied to back yard or garden.

Government Pamphlets

Write to Superintendent of Documents, Government Printing Office, Washington, D. C.

Attracting Birds, by W. L. McAtee. Conservation Bulletin No. 1. Fish and Wildlife Service. 10¢.

Covers feeders and bird baths and a little on planting to attract birds.

Food of Some Well-Known Birds of Forest, Farm and Garden by F. E. Beal. Farmers' Bulletin 506.

Fifty Common Birds of Farm and Orchard by F. E. Beal. Farmers' Bulletin 513.

Fruits Attractive to Birds, Northwestern States. Leaflet BS-41.

Fruits Attractive to Birds, Rocky Mountain States. Leaflet BS-42

Fruits Attractive to Birds, Northern Plains States. Leaflet BS-43

Fruits Attractive to Birds, Northeastern States. Leaflet BS-44

Fruits Attractive to Birds, California. Leaflet BS-45

Fruits Attractive to Birds, Great Basin States. Leaflet BS-46

Fruits Attractive to Birds, Southwestern States. Leaflet BS-47

Fruits Attractive to Birds, Southern Plains States. Leaflet BS-48

Fruits Attractive to Birds, Southeastern States. Leaflet BS-49

Fruits Attractive to Birds, Florida. Leaflet BS-50

(All of these BS-41 through BS-50, free from Department of Agriculture)

Homes for Birds by W. L. McAtee and E. R. Kalmach. Farmers' Bulletin 1456.

How to Attract Birds in Northeastern States. Farmers' Bull. 621.

How to Attract Birds in Northwestern States. Farmers' Bull. 760.

How to Attract Birds in Middle Atlantic States. Farmers' Bull. 844.

How to Attract Birds in East Central States. Farmers' Bull. 912.

(These four bulletins are 5¢ each)

FOR GENERAL READING

These books are suggested for pure entertainment, as well as for the information about birds that may be gained from the writings of these well-known birders.

Birds over America by Roger Tory Peterson. Dodd, Mead and Company, Inc., New York, N. Y.

Flight into Sunshine by Helen G. Cruickshank. The Macmillan Company, New York, N. Y.

Wild Birds at Home by Francis H. Herrick. Appleton-Century-Crofts, Inc., New York, N. Y.

Migration of American Birds by Frederick C. Lincoln. Doubleday and Company, Inc., Garden City, N. Y.

Bird Watching Days by A. W. P. Robertson and R. D. Powell. Collins, Publishers. London.

REGIONAL OR STATE BOOKS

Every birder will get a great deal of help from books or other publications on birds relating to his specific region or state. The following list is not too complete since many such publications were published many years ago and are now out of print, or otherwise unavailable, except perhaps in libraries. Some of the more recent books and pamphlets are listed here with the suggestion that those who do not find one listed for their area, look at one from neighboring regions or states.

Birds of Alabama by Arthur H. Howell. 1928. Department of Game and Fisheries, Montgomery, Alabama.

Birds of Arkansas by W. J. Baerg. 1931. University of Arkansas Experiment Station. Fayetteville, Ark.

Birds of California by W. L. Dawson. 1923. Various editions available. Check library files.

Guide to Colorado Birds by W. H. Bergtold. Smith-Brooks Printing Co., Denver, Col.

Florida Bird Life by Arthur H. Howell. National Audubon Society, 1000 Fifth Avenue, New York, N. Y.

Birds of Chicago Region by Ford, Sanford and Coursen. Chicago Academy of Science, Chicago, Ill.

Birds in Kansas by Arthur L. Goodrich. 1945. Kansas State Board of Agriculture, Topeka, Kansas.

Natural History of the Birds of Eastern and Central North America by E. H. Forbush, revised and abridged by John B. May. 1939. Houghton Mifflin Company, Boston, Mass.

Birds of Minnesota by Thomas S. Roberts. University of Minnesota Press, Minneapolis, Minn. 1937.

Bird Studies at Old Cape May (N. J.) by Witmer Stone. Delaware Valley Ornithological Club, Philadelphia, Pa.

Birds of New Mexico by Florence Merriam Bailey. 1928. New Mexico Department of Game and Fish, Santa Fe, N. M.

Birds Around New York City by Allan D. Cruickshank. American Museum of Natural History, New York, N. Y.

Birds of North Carolina by T. Gilbert Pearson and C. S. and H. H. Brimley. 1942. North Carolina Department of Agriculture, Raleigh, N. C.

Birds of Buckeye Lake, Ohio by Milton B. Trautman. 1940. University of Michigan, Ann Arbor, Mich.

Birds of Oklahoma by Margaret Morse Nice. 1931. University of Oklahoma, Norman, Okla.

Birds of Oregon by Ira N. Gabrielson and Stanley C. Jewett. 1940. Oregon State College, Corvallis, Ore.

Birds of Western Pennsylvania by W. E. Clyde Todd. 1940. University of Pittsburgh Press, Pittsburgh, Pa.

Wyoming Bird Life by Otto McCreary. 1937. University of Wyoming, Laramie, Wyo.

Birds of the Pacific States by Ralph Hoffmann. 1927. Houghton Mifflin Company, Boston, Mass.

Birds of Canada by P. A. Taverner. 1938. David McKay Company, Philadelphia, Pa.

GUIDES TO BIRD SONGS

American Bird Songs. An album of six double records, by the Albert R. Brand Bird Song Foundation. Comstock Publishing Company, Inc., Ithaca, N. Y. $8.50.

Record No. 1 (Both sides) Birds of the Northwoods

Record No. 2 (Both sides) Birds of Northern Gardens and Shade Trees

Record No. 3 (Both sides) Birds of Southern Woods and Gardens

Record No. 4 (Both sides) Birds of the Fields and Prairies

Record No. 5 (Both sides) North American Game Birds

Record No. 6 (Both sides) Birds of Western North America

A Guide to Bird Songs by Aretas A. Saunders. 1935. Appleton-Century-Crofts, Inc., New York, N. Y.

A good book for beginners when used as one listens to bird songs. Describes songs of 109 land birds of northeastern states.

INDEX